Feck O
Ya
Auld Eejit
Dublin Recollections

Bridget Griffiths

Bridan Publications

ISBN- 9798393107956

Cover design by: Siobhan Fogarty

Introduction

Thank you to the now deceased Sister Paul at St George's Hill in Dublin, who inspired Bridget, or Bridie as she was known, to believe in her writing abilities from a young age. This led her, in later life, to write this compendium of stories, drawn from her experience as a child growing up in the tenement blocks of north Dublin. These are tales of family, filled with humour, warmth, wit and sadness that tumbled from her distinctive Irish imagination. What a talent she had, and who knows what the same girl from a different background might have achieved. These fabulous stories, which met with critical acclaim on Facebook and beyond, are her legacy, providing a marvellous insight into the truly feckin' wonderful woman she was.

Wonderfully entertaining and moving snapshots of a way of life almost forgotten, seen through the eyes of an irrepressible, young Dubliner.
(Richard Attlee)

Contents

Chapter One
Ignorance is Bliss

I was born in the 1930's, so yes, a very tough time. But that old saying 'ignorance is bliss' comes to mind. As I remember, while growing up in the tenements, I was completely unaware of the deprivation, hunger and poverty that was happening all around me. A time that seemed to embody everything miserable. Going to the pawn shop was a norm, having a tick book was a norm, how was I to know we were marinated in the gravy train of despair? I thought everyone lived like that, unaware of the significance of it all. History was happening all around us, as would be shown by the many books on social history that would emerge many years later.

Books I read in older years that catapulted me back into my childhood and gave me an insight into the haves and have nots. I had never ventured far beyond the street where I lived. The first time I saw vast open fields was courtesy of the Vincent De Paul charity, with a trip to Balbriggan. I was a happy child playing skipping, beds and relieveo with my friends. Washing under a cold water tap in the backyard was normal, until Friday night when we had the luxury of a bath in the faithful old tin bath, in front of the fire. I can recall visiting a childhood friend whose family had just moved from the tenements to one of the first new corporation houses. The excitement at finding a whole new indoor toilet and wait for it...a 'proper' bath, was indescribable. Of course, we cried when we could not have the toys we wanted at Christmas or birthdays -I never remember having a birthday party but yet found delight in a Christmas stocking that contained a Cadbury's box, a couple of oranges and a shiny new 'thrupenny' piece. Looking back, and as children, how unaware we were of the trials and tribulations our dear parents were going through. Yet, through this rapid river of deprivation, from its sides and inlets, gently came meandering expressions of the human heart, bringing acts of sharing, helping, and above all caring for the older generation. I am an old woman now and thankfully share and know the warmth of a comfortable home. My two children have had a good education and will never know the fear projected by some of the nuns and brothers that I witnessed in my time. I never put a wash in a washing machine without thinking about and picturing my mam, washing in the old tin bath, a mountain of clothes by her feet and her fingers bleeding from use of the washing board. How I wish she had lived to see the wonders of today's technology, so life would have paled to what mam and the tenacious women of the tenements knew and suffered. So, yes, not the good old days by any means. However, I think we came away and left those times behind and took with us something money can't buy: to learn to live and cope in hard times, remembering kindness is the insignia of a loving heart, learning to share what little we have and remembering never to look down on anyone, as one day we may find ourselves looking up on them.

Chapter Two
A Star is Born

I knew from the age of seven that I was destined to be a star. After sitting through two showings of a Carmen Miranda picture in the Maro, or, should I say, 'The Mary Street Cinema', I was hooked. Just like a wriggling fish on the end of a fisherman's line! Open mouthed, I stared at the 'Brazilian Bombshell', as she flitted across the screen in her five-inch platform shoes and trade mark hat, adorned with a huge colourful collection of tropical fruit and plumes about two feet in height! But, even before that, I reasoned, had not the finger of fate pointed, not just once, but several times, indicating the path I should tread? How could I have missed the signs? Bless her, even my own mam must have had some inkling of the depth of talent buried within the squat (amend that to fat) frame of her schoolgirl daughter. Mind you, under the pressure of bringing up (then) eight children and looking after her own aged mother and father, on her own, sometimes the pressure exploded and brought forth the strangest phenomenal change of behaviour which resulted in name changes for us, her children! My beautiful sister Julia of the auburn curly hair became, 'ya red-headed so and so.' The youngest, May, became, 'crying bad luck.' I should mention the reason for this was as follows. Every Monday morning before we went to school Mam would check our hair for nits and 'fellas' for lice. May hated this and would cry through the whole procedure, even threatening mum. 'If ya find one I'll shake my head and it will get away.' Mam would shake her head and say, 'Ya cry bad luck into the house every Monday morning.' Hence the name. The boys were collectively known as, 'Wait till your da gets home.' They would have had to wait a very long time as Da was still in Italy, fighting in the war. And Michael? He remained just Michael, her darling boy. And I did not escape the wrath and sarcastic name calling, oh no. My sister would be told to go out and find 'the drama queen and tell her tea is ready.' Can you imagine my joy when after the story I am about to relate I was promoted to, 'go find the mad actress.' Yes indeed, recognition at last, my day had arrived!

It did not bother me my sisters were so much prettier than I. They may have had the looks whereas I, to my mind, was blessed with a talent for acting and singing and a confidence that knew no bounds! I had always had a vivid imagination, as already proven by the English compositions I submitted at school, always walking off with the first prize of a holy picture! People had got to Hollywood on talent alone, I reasoned. Just look at Katherine Hepburn, imbued with an acting talent that left her beautiful co-stars way behind. Other incidents came to the fore, as I reflected on the awareness and awakening of my newly found talent. Why, for instance, when playing ball, if the ball was 'canted' (lost), was I the one always sent to plead for its return from some auld rip? Did my small companions recognise the pathos, humility and sorrowful face and actions I adopted, just to get the fecking auld ball back? Yes indeed, that was it! Even these children knew greatness when they saw it! And, again, only last week, had not the choir mistress over in Halson Street Church told me I had a lovely voice and, to prove it, given me the solo spot at Mass singing Panis Angelicus? I had found the perfect 'studio' to practice in and help bring forth this superb talent that had lain dormant within me.

Me granny's little back bedroom was only used at night and, not only that, but wasn't it grand! She had a full-length mirror! Ah, sure, I was made up.

Day after day, I practised the 'Aye, aye, aye I like you very much' song from the movie, not only perfecting the South

American accent, but also the exaggerated hand movements and, most importantly, the rolling of the eyes! I searched through Granny's wardrobe seeking something bright and colourful to match Carmen's dress, but should have known better. Granny only ever wore black. I did however find Granddad's brown trilby hat, the one he wore with his brown suit. I still hadn't solved the problem of how to adorn me auld Granddad's hat! Granny and Granddad were still below talking to Mam when I slipped into their pristine larger room. My eyes covered that room before coming to rest on Granny's prized side board, the one the Jewish gentleman always wanted to buy. The side board carried three large shades, the end ones carrying statues of the Sacred Heart and the Blessed Virgin. But the centre shade held an array of tropical birds of vibrant colours. I whispered a prayer of thanks to St. Anthony, he had found what I wanted. My eccentric Aunt Bridget, Mam's sister was surely right when she informed me, 'Ah, sure he's a grand fella, he will always find things that are lost.' In my case I was stretching things a bit! I climbed onto a chair and, with great difficulty, removed the very heavy shade, but no matter how hard I pulled, I could not remove the feathers from the birds. Jumping from the chair, I entered the small closet in the corner of the room, my grandfather's workshop and there among the welts, awls, uppers and all the other paraphernalia required in the making of shoes, I found what I was seeking! A pair of scissors. Back onto the chair, where I discovered that while I could cut and detach the spine, nothing came away complete! I also noticed lots of coloured 'dust' adorning Granny's prized sideboard! The actual feathers just disintegrated and why had I the feeling the eyes of both statues appeared to be following my every movement, as if to say, 'serves you right'. I had by now spoiled several birds and endeavoured to cover the damage by spreading the feathers of the 'healthy' birds over the damaged ones, but they just sprang back into place. I turned the shade around hiding the damage at the back.

10

Years later, I would leave home and up to that time no one had noticed anything amiss with Granny's birds and I was not about to point it out! Granny's eyesight was rapidly failing, so I blamed that, or otherwise she never dusted very often! Finally, I had to make do with one of me Ma's towels, twisting it into a turban. Ma's eccentric sister, Auntie Bridget, gave me a brooch which I pinned to the front and sure it looked really grand. I looked the part! I couldn't wait for the nice bright evenings when, after tea, all the auld grannies and the mas would come to the front door of the tenements with an array of orange boxes, stools, and chairs, the latter usually with no backs to them. They would gather and sit in small groups and gossip about the days happenings, while keeping an eye on us kids. When boredom set in, they would usually extend an invitation to the kids. 'Why don't yez come over and sing an auld song or do a dance, do anything and we'll give the winner a penny and the rest of ya some fruit.' The fruit offer always came from the dealers who sold in Moore Street, as many of them lived in our street. We needed no second bidding and would end up elbowing each other out of the way, in our bid to perform and win that coveted penny. As usual, snotty nosed Billy would be first on the queue, with his whistling act. I swear he fancied himself as an expert on bird calls, another Ronnie Ronald in the making. I leaned on the railings, watching, praying he would not win! I still felt me face go red at the dirty auld trick he had played on me, only the week before. Nancy and I had met him on our way to school. Not only was he eating an apple, but also had a bag of sweets in his hand. He boasted about a rich uncle who was visiting from the States. 'Me rich uncle gave us all half a crown each.' he crowed. Nancy and I had looked at each other, our eyes popping out of our heads. 'Go away with ya! He never.' sez Nancy. 'I'll prove it to ya, do yez want sixpence.' he asked? 'Jaysus, are yer joking! Course we do.' 'Right, you'll have to put your hand in me pocket to get it, cause me hands are full.'

11

Like a fool, I put me hand into his trouser pocket to discover, not only no sixpence, but no lining either! Boys did not wear underpants way back then! 'Go way ya little dirt bird.' I cried, me face red with embarrassment. Me and Nancy sent him on his way after giving him a good boxing round the ears. I had now reached the top of the line of performing hopefuls. My big moment had arrived. Of course, I had run indoors to fetch my Carmen Miranda turban. 'I hope that's not me good towel, I only use that for the hospital,' sniffed me Ma, as I passed her chair. How, I wondered, could Ma think of something as mundane as an auld towel when I, her daughter, was about to enter the world of show business? I was about to make my début and did not have a nervous bone in my body, as I faced my family, shawl clad neighbours, their children and children's, children. Even the auld mongrel dogs of the street lazily opened their eyes, from where they were lay, as if in protest, as the first notes of my 'ay, ay, ay, I like you very much', rang out. I wanted my 'performance' to be perfect and so, made every effort with my hand movements, rolling my eyes until they almost popped out of their sockets! How hard I had worked on that accent, wanting to perfect it, until I sounded like a native Brazilian just like my idol, Carmen. I was about half way through my 'performance' before I noticed it! Cough, cough, first one and then another, but at least they had the decency to bring the shawl and coat collars up above their faces to muffle the sound and not distract or spoil my performance! But why, I wondered, did their bodies appear to be shaking beneath the coats and shawls? More noise, TUT! First, one auld one arose, leaving to rush into the tenement hall door behind her, followed by yet another. What was that noise I was hearing? Giggling? Laughter? Surely not? I took the opportunity, during a pause in the song, to glance at my Ma, only to see tears streaming down her eyes and worryingly she too appeared to have been struck down with this strange malady that, like the others, caused her whole body

12

to shake! I finished my song to much applause and, after a short discussion, I was voted the winner and presented with the much coveted penny! I would go on to win the penny for many more weeks of these impromptu talent competitions, until in the end I became fed up by the coughing fits and shaking bodies my voice appeared to induce! I knew I had the best voice in the choir, the choir mistress had told me so on more than one occasion. Undeterred, I strove to achieve my ambition, still blithely unaware and ignorant of the laughter the sight of my fat little body doing a dreadful imitation of a Brazilian bombshell had caused! 'Ma, can I have the money for a stamp please.' 'What would ya be wanting a stamp for?' 'I want to write a letter to the Queen's.' 'Holy Mother of God! What would ya be doing writing to the Queen?' 'No Ma, not THE QUEEN! I mean The Queen's Concert Hall.' 'What would ya be writing to them for?' 'Ma, I'm writing away for an application form to enter the Sunday night competition.' 'Ah, no! Don't tell me we're all going through that again. I'm telling ya, you're a mad actress.' 'Yes, Ma, I know. Isn't it grand.' I smiled. There must have been an awful lot of talent in Dublin all those years ago. It was weeks before I got an answer to my application to enter the talent competition at the 'Queen's'. Mind ya, I got value for money from that letter, flashing it around school, as though it were a ticket to Hollywood. Of course, people didn't get to look at it just like that! (Snaps fingers) This precious document could only be viewed on payment with any of the following: four licks of a lolly, two caramels or six dolly mixture (cause they are so tiny), the butt of a green apple (a large one), or some liquorice bark. Why, even Miss O'Malley the choir mistress got to hear of my forthcoming adventure! 'Is it true Bridget, that you're going to enter a talent competition?' 'Yes, miss, it is.' 'You will be singing, of course?' 'Yes, I will, miss.' (Thinks) What the feck did she think I was gonna do, hand stands? 'That's lovely Bridget, I've no doubt you will walk away with it, and sure how many times have I said you have a beautiful voice?' Red face. 'Err, thank you, miss.' As she spoke, I could see Maeve Malone hovering just beyond her shoulder. I could tell by the look on her face she was only bulling (annoyed) because I had got some praise. I had to admit, she was a grand singer, but now I'm not being big headed, but everyone said I was far better than her! I had long discussions with my reluctant musical director, our eccentric Aunt Bridget. Every time she called down to see her sister, (me mam) I cornered her, seeking advice on what number I should perform. I had intended doing me Carmen Miranda number, but Bridget thought it might be a bit too sophisticated for the Queen's! Well, to be honest, she didn't use that big word. What she actually said it was a load of shit, which surprised me as she was a real Holy Mary who never swore. Now, my Ma on the other hand, well, I better not even go there. 'Listen, Alanna, (she always called me that), would ya not like to sing the Ave Maria or, even the Panis Angelicus?, she asked. 'Sure, ya make a grand job of them, brings tears to me eyes!' 'No, every one sings the Ave Maria. I don't want to do that.' I started to have doubts as to my choice of musical director. Auntie Bridget's ability or lack of it became glaringly apparent the nearer we got to the competition. What would I sing? We decided, or, should I say she decided, on a song that I had never heard of, nor as it turned out, had anyone else. I spent all my spare time practising this song in me granny's little bedroom, away from prying eyes! Now, I really panicked when I heard Granny singing along with the song one day. If Granny knew it, it must be old! Sure, Granny was at least seventy-three, if not more. After almost seventy years, the words are SEARED (I don't use that word lightly) into my brain! Part of it is as follows: We'll meet again by the roses In the valley of the moon We kissed and said good bye You cried and so did I And now you wonder why I'm lonely We'll meet again by the roses in the valley of the moon. (Yawnsssssssssssssssssssssssssss) Holy Mother of God! Can you imagine a seven year old stood on a stage singing that!

God! It's a good job no member of the 'cruelty to children' department was around, sure they would have charged me Ma with cruelty and taken me away from her. I was becoming temperamental, as befits a future star of stage and yes, why not, maybe even screen! 'I'll need a new dress and what about me hair?' I constantly berated my poor unfortunate mother! 'You'll wear you're communion dress and I'll put a few rags in your hair.' replied my Ma with a look that boded trouble, were I to proceed with my ranting and raving! At least I got a new pair of runners from Casey's, a little drapers shop in Bolton Street. My Auntie Bridget bought me a pair of white socks to go with them. I decided not to 'push' too much for the dress; I knew if Ma lost her temper I wouldn't be going anywhere. My communion dress was pretty enough in its simplicity, so I didn't feel I should expect to hear 'Queen of the May' as I walked out on stage. The night before the concert Ma cut an old sheet into long strips and, after she had washed my hair, deftly proceeded to wrap the strips both downwards then upwards around my long hair, before tying them in place near the scalp. I ended up looking like an emergency case for the A and E department of Jervis Street hospital! Imagine! A child's head, with what looked like a hundred bandaged fingers protruding from its scalp! After a tortuous night of lying on what felt like a sack of carrots, I have to admit I had a massive head of long ringlets, when the rags were removed the following morning. Ah, (sigh), what we show business people endure for the sake of our art! Standing by the side of the stage with about eight other kids, I could already feel the heat of the stage lighting burning my face. One of the smaller boys had already wet himself with fright, leaving a small pool on the floor, much to the anger of the man in charge of us! I myself was trembling, as I watched my fellow contestants go out on to the vast stage, as their names were called. So far there had been one recitation, a pair of tap dancers, an accordion player and, oh, Lord! they were calling my name! 'Err; I

15

need to go to the lavatory,' I whispered to the man in charge of us. 'Not now ya don't,' he whispered fiercely in a deep country accent. He pushed me out on to the stage. The walk from the side of the stage to its centre felt like a mile. I looked out into the darkness hoping to see my Ma, siblings, and the one or two neighbours who had come to cheer me on. All I could make out, through a haze of smoke, were the people in the first couple of rows and Ma was among them. Behind me and to the left hand side of the stage was a piano. The man seated there gave a slight cough to draw my attention and, as I looked at him, a slight nod to indicate I should start to sing my song. I opened my mouth and nothing came out! Again, he went through the introduction notes and, thankfully from somewhere, out came the words: 'we'll meet again by the roses.' I soon realized the pianist was unfamiliar with the song and, who could blame him, it was so old. He was following me, but was a few bars behind through most of the song. I was bloody petrified and, almost ran off the stage when I had finished to lukewarm applause. Another name was called and, I know not from where, came the next contestant. I had not even noticed her in the line up. A lovely dainty young girl with a beautiful head of blonde curls, ones I could tell at a glance that were not the result of 'rags'. At least, she had been assured of a good night's sleep! The hair was topped off with the biggest bow I had ever seen. She wore a beautiful, short, pink dress similar in shape to that of a ballerina and, on her feet, matching shoes. Her feet hardly touched the floor as she smilingly made her way on to the stage. 'Ah, feck! Not her,' said a voice behind me. I looked around at the speaker, a red-headed boy with freckles galore. 'Why, what do ya mean?' I whispered. 'Well, we might as well all feck off home, we've no chance of winning once she's here.' Nodding in the girl's direction, he continued, 'Your one's from Gardiner Street and she has a big crowd following and clapping her, that's how she always wins.' he explained in a disgruntled voice. As if to prove a point, the applause was

16

thunderous as the girl crossed the stage, even before she had opened her mouth to sing. While she did not have a strong voice, she did have a very sweet one. Even from where I was standing on the side of the stage, I was struck by (and envied) her wonderful self-assurance. The format was as follows. As soon as all the contestants had performed, they would line up on stage. The theatre manager would pass behind, placing his hand over each head. The audience would clap for their favourite act. The child who received the greatest applause was the winner. Wouldn't ya just know it!! I was placed right beside the little doll like girl, her daintiness making me stand out like Jack, of the beanstalk story! As predicated by 'freckle face', the applause almost brought the roof down when the hand was placed over the girl's head, while at the same time her name was being screamed from the cavernous darkness of the theatre. I myself received just 'fair' applause and I would say, even that, was a generous sympathy vote. Ma and our family picked me up from the stage door and I could see they were treading cautiously, thinking they were going to find me in disappointed floods of tears. Even my normally "rough and tumble" brothers had come over all soft, while assuring me, 'Yer one should never have won, I swear ya sang better than her.' 'Yeah! Your right there, sham' sez brother number two. 'And if it wasn't for her big gang of followers she would never have won. Sure, even that specky eyed kid on the accordion was better than her.' Ma squeezed my hand trying to reassure me that 'never mind', everything was going to be all right. And, as if to make up for any disappointment... 'I know. Let's go to Benny's Chippy and we'll get a couple of one and ones and share them. What do ya say to that?' 'Ma, when we go into Benny's, can I order?' I asked. 'Why? What for?' 'Well, do ya remember when me Da taught us a few words of Italian? Well, I just want to practise me accent and acting on Benny'. Ma pulled up sharply and, looking down at me, shook her head as she said, 'Now, for God's sake, don't tell me we have to go

17

through all that again!' A life time later... I was sat in the world-famous theatre of The Royal Shakespeare Company in Stratford-upon-Avon. From my lofty position, I watched the actors and one in particular. It was a very hot summer. I was really enjoying the play, but was glad of the chance to get outside for a breath of fresh air during the interval. Because of the crowds, one could not help but overhear the conversations of the people all around. First man: 'What an excellent play, and what wonderful acting.' Second man: 'Yes, I certainly do agree with you. I was particularly struck by the young actress playing the part of Lady Eitherside. I thought she was outstanding.' First man: 'Yes, I noticed her too, a fine young actress.'

They moved on and the rest of the conversation was lost to me. The urge to chase after them, grab their arm and proudly say to them, 'That's my girl you're talking about' was strong, but I resisted. It was in the genes, was it not? And, of course, she got it from her Mum! Who else?

Chapter Three
My Nemesis

Morning prayers were over and we children had made our
way back to our respective class rooms, ready to begin yet
another day at school. I just can't remember how old I was.
We stood up from our desks as Sister Mary Bishop entered
the room, and resumed sitting only when we were given the
nod to do so. She carried a large stack of exercise books
which she then placed on the table in front of her. Placing
her two forefingers to the side of her face, (the only part of
her showing), she pushed the white wimple back from
where it was biting into her skin. She was a very tall,
heavyset woman dressed from head to toe in the black habit
of the Presentation Sisters, the heavy skirts reaching down
to her ankles, just allowing a glimpse of the thick black
stockings and heavy black shoes peeking from beneath its
folds. Even from my desk at the back of the class, I
recognized my own exercise book on top of the pile. I loved
to get a new book and would take great care lovingly
covering its outer cover with nice brown paper, before
carefully writing my name on it. I would flick through the
empty book, promising myself never to get an ink blot or
finger mark on its virgin pages. I felt really proud of this
particular book, feeling I had really excelled myself. In this
instance, not for me any old common or garden brown
paper, oh no!
After our room was decorated, how delighted I was to find
there was some wallpaper left over, enough to cover mine
and my sisters school books. And there, atop the teachers
table, the great big cabbage roses of the wall paper shone
out (to me) like the beam of a lighthouse at sea. In those far

off days, we would be given an English exercise to do and be expected to fulfil the required four or five hundred words. A title such as, 'I am a plane', 'I am a motor car', or such like, would be given and we would be expected to carry on from there. How I loved doing these, having a vivid imagination I never had any trouble finding things to write about. I would rush home from school and go straight to Nana's room, where I would sit at her polished round table and in the glow of the gas light, I would put my head down and, as in the case of 'I am a plane', enter a world of metal, rivets, screws and workforces. Not for me, 'I am a plane, I fly in the sky and carry passengers all over the world.' Oh no, that was too easy! My particular plane had to be 'born' from scratch, its progress accounted for from start to finish! I would describe the new plush seats, its interior, and yes, even down to the uniforms of the pilot and air hostesses. Of course, in the end, my plane would eventually crash, but not before it had given great service as a passenger plane and, eventually a war plane, after a huge conversion! I could not write the words down fast enough, the ideas tumbling from my child's mind, as fast as water from a tap! Sister Mary Bishop raised her eyes from the table, carefully studying each face before finally coming to rest on mine. 'Bridget, come to the top of the class.' I felt my face go red, I hated being brought to the front of the class, feeling the eyes of my school friends bore into my back, as I reluctantly made my way there. I reached her table, just as she reached out and removed my book from the top of the pile. 'Is this your book?'

'Yes, Sister, it is.' (I wondered was I in trouble on account of my beautiful wallpaper covering). 'How long did it take you to write this exercise?' 'Err, I don't really know, I went home, but my brothers were sat at our kitchen table doing their homework, so I went upstairs to Nana's rooms to do mine.

Nana gave me some hot cocoa and after that I started writing and did not stop until I had finished my exercise.'

'Pray tell me, who helped you with your homework?' 'Why, nobody helped me Sister, I did it by myself.' 'Don't lie to me, I want the truth.' 'I am telling the truth.' 'If nobody helped you, then where did you copy it from?' 'I did not copy it from anyone. I did it by myself, just ask my Nana.' 'Why did you exceed the five hundred words I set?' 'Er, I'm not sure what you mean, Sister".' 'I mean, why did you go over five hundred words?' 'Sister, I just could not fit in all I wanted to write in five hundred words.' (In a raised voice) 'I want the truth'. At this point, and almost in tears, I proceeded to do what every Dublin child did when they were trying to convince someone they were telling the truth. Wetting my forefinger against my tongue, I placed the finger against my Adam's apple and making the sign of the cross said: 'I swear to God, I am telling the truth. 'Not only lying, but taking the Lord's name in vain.' Opening the table drawer, she removed the 'slapper', which was almost identical to the butter pats the dairies used to pat butter into shape. 'Hold out your hand.' I held out my right hand, palm upwards and winced as the 'slapper' came down heavily three times! 'Now the other one.' Holding out my left hand I received another 'three of the best'. By now, the tears I had tried to suppress came rolling down my cheeks and I was ordered back to my desk. I walked slowly back, a hand under each armpit, trying to ease the pain in my stinging palms. Mammy was ironing, as usual, when I arrived home from school. 'Oh mammy I got killed (childish Dublin expression) today in school by Sister Mary Bi—op'. 'And what did you get killed for?' 'For nothing, mammy, I did nothing.' 'Will you go on out of that, you must have done something. The good sisters don't slap you for nothing.' I went up to Nana's room, but got no sympathy there either 'You must have done something wrong. Were you a bold (naughty) girl?' Our family were sent to school clean and tidy every day, me with two long plaits pulled back so tightly, it resulted in an instant facelift! Our attendance was excellent (apart from sickness) in all. We were well behaved, knowing we would have Da to answer to if it were otherwise! Time after time it was impressed upon us how important it was to learn the Irish language. 'You will never get a job in any government department or the post office unless you learn the Irish language, 'we were constantly told. On passing the exam for the Irish language, one was presented with a gold coloured lapel pin in the shape of a ring. It was called a 'Faine'. Alas, the nearest I ever got to this was my own wedding ring. No matter how hard I tried, I simply could not grasp the Irish language and, likewise, arithmetic. I was doing all right, until I got to decimal points and again, could not grasp it. History, Geography and English I loved, that was, until the above related incident regarding my exercise. I lost all confidence, frightened to submit work in case I was accused of cheating or copying from books. Even at that young age, I had no illusions about getting a grand job in some government department or the post office; I just was not clever enough. Because of one stupid incident, my greatest passion, English, was snatched away from me. Never again would I be able to open my book and lose myself in a world of my own making, with the aid of my trusty pen and bottle of ink. We were short of material things because of circumstances. Had not my late brother, Michael, lost his dream to go on to further education, because the family could not afford the books and uniform? While his dream had been snatched away, I knew that I would never have to face such a dilemma, his had been a brilliant mind. I was very happy in my own way, (apart from Irish and maths), knowing I could take myself off to Nana's room and lose myself in a book or writing. And so, I regressed, rather than progressed, and lost a lot of tuition along the way, afraid to stand up in class or even put my hand up to answer questions I knew the answers to. I would sadly have yet another 'run-in' with Sister Mary Bishop.

I was in the classroom of Miss M when she ran out of chalk for the blackboard. She picked on me to go to the next door classroom and get some chalk from the teacher there. I went and politely knocked on the door, until a voice bid me, 'Come in.' On entering, to my horror I found the teacher was Sister M. I approached her and said, 'Please Sister, can Miss M have some...' and that was as far as I got! She lifted her hand striking me so hard across the face, I ended up on the other side of the room! 'You will never approach me without first saying, excuse me.'

I was mortified that this had happened in front of a classroom full of younger pupils! Even now, in old age, these two incidents are embedded in my mind as plain as the handprint she left on my face. I am at pains here to impress upon anyone reading this that all the Sisters did not have the cruel streak possessed by Sister M. Who knows what caused her to be like this? Did she have worries and problems we knew nothing about? In what would be my last year, I would be lucky to have the most wonderful Sister Paul as my teacher. This lady dedicated her life to teaching the children from the slums of North Dublin, her patience, tenacity and ongoing enthusiasm lighting up the whole school. She must have seen some little spark in me, encouraging me no end, especially in English, but by then it was too late. I would leave school just before my 14th birthday and start work as a machinist in a factory where they made raincoats. I would never lose touch with her writing and telling her of my marriage and children and all the events happening in my life. I managed to visit her at the retirement home for nuns on one of my rare visits home. How sad I was to see she was by now badly crippled with arthritis and could only shuffle along with the help of a walking frame. Some years later, on yet another visit, I wrote and told her I would be again visiting her on the twelfth of May. She passed away on the tenth of that month. She was then ninety years of age. Making my way to the retirement home, I was directed to the small cemetery where the nuns were buried. I stood looking down at the still new mound of earth, before placing the flowers on top. As I stood there thinking of this gentle soul who had changed the lives of so many of the pupils who had passed through her hands over the years, I whispered a prayer of thanks. How grateful I was that the strands of her life had interwoven with mine, a child of the tenements, even for a short time.

Chapter Four
Will I Tell Ya A Story?

The sands of time have swiftly flown through the hour glass, and with it our trials and tribulations! Our family have grown up and are now scattered, with children of their own. I have jumped forward through the years and my now aged parents have long since left Dublin and are living near me in a city in England. I was hot and sweaty, as I pulled/dragged the heavy hoover from my house to Ma's. I muttered a few choice expletives under my breath and took great delight imagining the expression on my Da's face as I did so!! He never swore, despite having worked as a docker and after that, many years in the army, having reached the rank of sergeant. On the rare occasion he took the Lord's name in vain, he would immediately apologise. It appalled him to hear a woman swear. This ritual with the hoover was carried out almost every other day, and all down to Da's refusal to buy Ma a new one! How, I wondered, could two people be so different and still be together after fifty odd years of marriage? As mentioned in earlier 'recollections', my Ma was the soul of generosity, always willing to share what little she had with less fortunate neighbours, in our street of now demolished houses back home. My Da, on the other hand, was the complete opposite. Our darling Ma's love knew no bounds and she demonstrated this in a thousand ways, while my Da ruled the home with a discipline more suited to an army barracks. He was a man of that era, a time when an Irishman would not be caught dead pushing a baby in a pram, Oh no, that was a woman's work, as well as the

washing, cooking, and all the other many jobs that entailed raising a large family! Even at this late stage, I doff an imaginary hat to the very few men of our street who helped in their homes but, alas, be it secretly! All of our large family toed the line where Da was concerned, well, almost all! By the time I reached my late teens I rebelled and stood up to Da, rebelling at what I saw as injustices or unfairness to my beloved Ma. I cannot honestly say he was mean with money, but he lived in a world where he thought prices remained the same and the housekeeping allowance he gave Ma remained the same for many years, despite increases in rent and the cost of living. If, for instance, Ma needed a new coat, my brothers and sisters would get together muttering and arguing as to which one of us was going to approach Da and ask for it! Without fail I was always elected with the words, 'Let Bridget ask, she is not afraid to approach him', and this from my older siblings! After many hours of practising my approach, before entering the lion's den (and too young to have a drink to sustain me), I would venture forward into the arena, flying the flag for Ma and her new coat!! 'Da, don't you think it's about time Ma had a new coat?' 'Why? What's wrong with the one she has?' 'Well, it is rather shabby and the last time that style was in vogue, Mrs Simpson was wearing it.' 'Who's Mrs Simson? Was she the woman from Capel Street back home who collected for the Vincent de Paul?' '"No Da, she was the woman a King gave up his throne for. All I'm asking you for is a coat.'
Da, now spluttering with shock: 'I bought your mother a new coat when we went on holidays.' I point out that famous one and only holiday to Germany took place some five years ago, (courtesy of our brother), when we almost had to use thumb screws on Da to outfit Ma for the occasion! Reluctantly, I am given the go-ahead to buy the coat. He is unaware that I have already bought Ma a new coat, which is now secretly stashed away in my wardrobe, and several days later I produce and bill him for the coat, adding several pounds to the price.

The cries of, 'HOW MUCH', can be heard in the neighbouring borough!! I pacify him by telling him it should have cost a great deal more, but as I knew the girl in the shop, I got a great discount! How delighted I was to be able to pass the money on to Ma. She never spent it on herself, but would send it on to a younger sister back home who was struggling with a young family. I never had any qualms or feelings of guilt about this. Da called at his local every evening for a couple of drinks on his way home from work, and was not averse to buying all and sundry a drink. I reasoned it was better for Ma to have it than his drinking cronies. I even encouraged Ma to sneak a pound or two from his pockets when he came home, the worse for wear! Honesty was the name of the game as far as Ma was concerned. She would not steal a penny from Da, no matter how tipsy he got. He, Da, boasted that no matter how inebriated he was, he would know, down to the last penny, how much should be in his pocket the following morning! What a bluffer! Despite our differences, Da and I had a healthy respect for each other. I was always very upfront, telling him in no uncertain way what I thought, even if this resulted in an argument, which it invariably did! While I abhorred his tightness with money,   I admired his courage and tenacity, also his brilliant work ethic. Having lost a leg on the 25th of January from an industrial accident, he was back at work in March of the same year, despite excruciating pain adjusting to the artificial leg. He was awarded the grand sum of £2,000 for that accident. I think that was in 1960. This, of course, enabled them to leave Dublin and move to the U.K. We, their family and grandchildren, were already here apart from one brother and sister who wished to stay in Dublin. I did all I could to help Ma and Da even down to decorating their 3 bedroom house on my own, fitting it in, while on shift work, including nights. While Ma was horrified and feeling guilty at this mammoth task, Da took it in his stride, expecting it of me. He would never say, 'I wonder if you could possibly do this for me', but rather, 'I want you to sort out some problem or other'. With both well into old age, I was by now well versed in his ways, and in a perverse sort of way, felt that despite our many clashes over the years, I was the one he turned to as his 'port in a storm'. And yet another morning of lugging my hoover around to Ma's to help with her cleaning. Always a fastidious woman and despite her age, she still loved her home to be spick and span. On this particular morning we tackled all the downstairs area, before venturing upstairs to change the bedding and clean the bedrooms. At this stage in their lives, they each had their own bedroom. I suggested Ma 'do' her room, while I did Da's. As mentioned previously, Da had an artificial leg, and also a spare one, in case of emergencies! The 'spare' stood in his bedroom, complete with shoe and sock, (no! don't even go there!). On entering Da's bedroom, I never could manage to suppress the laughter this sight evoked in me! Racing against the clock to make sure I was in time for my work shift, I hurriedly set about my task and in doing so knocked over the spare leg!! As long as I live, I shall never forget the sight that met me as I bent to straighten it up!

There, tumbling from within its' hollow cavity, were large numbers of pound notes and five pound notes. I could not believe what I was seeing; my Da's secret bank and I had stumbled upon it by accident! My hysterical laughter brought Ma rushing in from her bedroom. She almost fainted with shock at the sight, and this belonged to a man who had complained he could not afford to buy a new hoover! There must have been about two hundred pounds, a fortune in those far off days. After the shock came the anger, on my part at least, my mind recalling the many occasions I had to wheedle and cajole to get him to change or buy something for the house. Ma, even went as far as to utter the immortal words, 'Well, the tight old bugger', and believe me, that was something that creased me up so much I was hysterical with laughter! We both ended up on the floor, laughing so much we were unable to talk, tears streaming down our eyes and holding our aching sides. 'You see,' I pointed out to Ma, 'despite your protestations, I was right to add a pound here and there when I had to bill Da for something! The end justified the means.' Ma almost fainted on the spot, when I suggested we remove enough money to buy a new hoover! With hand on heart, I can honestly say I have never done a dishonest act in my life, well, apart from the time I stole a hairnet from Woolworths, to give to Ma on Mother's Day. Oh yes, I almost forgot to mention about adding a couple of pounds to Da's bills, but did the end not justify the means? In this particular instance, I looked at my wonderful little Ma and like the trailer for an old black and white movie, scenes flashed before my eyes. The farce we went through to get Ma a new coat, the times we had asked for money towards the decorating with the usual reply, 'Where do you think I would get the money.' So many little unpleasant memories which, when woven together, formed a blanket of selfishness, worthy of my Da's shoulders! No, I felt not one iota of shame as I calmly removed fifty pounds from his secret stash! Poor Ma was in a state of collapse at my audacity and I didn't put it back, despite her protest of, 'He will go mad, there will be murder.' I smugly carried out my dastardly deed with, I might add, much glee at the thought of a lot less pints at the local bar. We, or should I say I, bided my time waiting for the roof to cave in and after a week, not a sound or a bellow. My Da had bluffed for so many years, telling all who were prepared to listen, that no matter how drunk he got, he could tell if a penny was missing from his pocket!! Well, fifty pounds was now missing from his pocket, or should I say his leg (LOL) and he was not even aware of it!! I waited another week before going to the shop and buying Ma a reconditioned hoover which cost £25. As already stated, Ma was such an honest and devout woman, she could not live with the guilt of my dastardly act! I have to admit, I was angry when she confessed to putting the remaining £25 back in 'the leg'. Da's secret bank he had never missed it. The following year would see her donate a £1 every week in the church poor box, until she had repaid the stolen £25, we had paid for the hoover, which, by the way, was trouble from day one! Poetic justice, eh? 'Ma, why did you do that, you needed it more than Da!' 'Well, I confessed it in confession and the priest told me it should be repaid. I could hardly hand it back to your father now, could I? I was so worried, wondering where I was going to get £25, but Father said under the circumstances I should put a sum into the poor box every week, until the full sum was paid'. Was it any wonder I loved and adored my darling Mammy? I loved and respected my father. I admired his courage and work ethic, but wished he had moved forward with the times, even a little.

Chapter Five
Tragedy

I don't know why but, I never considered Ireland to be an animal loving nation. Perhaps that was because, many years later, in another place and another time I would witness, to my amazement, the lavish love and attention bestowed by owners on their pets. On reflection, of course mine was an unfair assumption! I never remembered seeing a tin of dog or cat meat and, why should I? God, families were struggling to try and feed themselves, never mind the animals. Of course, they, the dogs did not go hungry but were fed from table scraps and a few bones and innards boiled up in an old pot on the gas stove. These would have been obtained from the slaughterhouse that was part of the complex of Coles Lane. Without exception I cannot ever remember entering a street of Dublin tenements without encountering a pack of roaming mongrel dogs of all shapes and colours. So, I guess there were some animal lovers amongst us after all! In my own street of twenty-seven houses at least twelve dogs belonged to various families. Now, when you think each house was home to at least five families and, sometimes more, that wasn't too bad!! Some were harmless while others were vicious brutes to be avoided at all costs. Surely, it was only the with and "tongue in cheek" of a Dubliner who could have thought up the names of some of these dogs! "Sooner" because it would sooner shit than bark "Floozie" because of the amount of times it had to be separated from other dogs! "Rasher" who, despite being fed was all skin and bone. "Black Bomber" named after the black boxer Joe Lewis. These are just a few of those I can remember. Our own dog was simply Rex and the following relates to his time in our family. The two small boys were still arguing as they left Loftus Lane, crossed over Parnell Street and entered the familiar surroundings of their own street. Mike, the older, but smaller of the two turned this way and that trying to avoid the hands of his younger, but taller brother Paddy as he, endeavoured to reach the hidden object under Mike's coat. On reaching home, my Da's voice shouting, "What's going on?" brought the squabble to a swift close. And so the story unfolded as each boy gave their version of what had happened. Cutting through what we kids called William & Woods Lane on their way home, their attention was drawn to a sack tied with a rope. From within came tiny whimpering sounds which caused the boys to draw closer. Paddy undid the rope and taking the two end corners, gingerly tipped the contents on the ground. Lying there, shivering and frightened was the smallest puppy they had ever seen. Mike gently lifted it and placed it under his coat where it would hopefully get some body heat. Now the question arose, whose dog was it? Both boys wanted to claim it as their own! My Da listened as each of my brothers gave their reasons as to why they should be the owner, Paddy putting forward the valid argument it would still be there in the lane had he not opened the sack. Mike's answer to that was that he was the first to pick it up and probably saved its life by keeping it warm". Eyeing this tiny scrap of a puppy he humoured the boys, convinced that it would not survive until morning. Da then suggested that he would toss a coin and whichever boy called correctly would own the dog. Paddy agreed to this but Mike was adamant he would have no part of it, the thought of not owing the dog sat poorly on his shoulders! Mike was born with a heart defect. He was not a strong robust boy as were others of the same age.

While he and Paddy fought continually, they were inseparable. Paddy would take on and fight any boy who took advantage of Mike's slight frame. Graciously, Paddy agreed to Mike having the dog. Had the tossing of a coin taken place and, had Paddy won, in reality, he would have walked away the loser. Fate and the new addition to our family decided who was to be its master from day one! Sitting in front of the glowing embers to keep it warm, Mike and Paddy sat up most of the night feeding the puppy warm milk and "pops" The puppy was given the name Rex. He would forever follow Mike. Dad's prediction that the puppy would not last the night couldn't have been more wrong! Rex was to be part of our family for the next eighteen years, sadly outliving his young owner. Rex was already a part of the household when I and younger siblings were born. He became our pet; he would let us pull him around and ride on his back with never a snarl or bark. As youngsters, my sisters and I would dress him up, wrapping him into an old shawl and bonnet. We struggled to lift and place him in the home made buggy before proceeding to wheel him up and down our street. He passively lay there, allowing us to do so! Mike would get so angry when he found us using his dog as a dolly, claiming we were turning Rex into a "Sissy" dog! A great house dog, he recognized all the family footsteps as we entered the hall and would wag his tail. If a stranger entered the open hall door he would bark like mad. A mongrel, black and tan in colour, he followed Mike everywhere, even to school, waiting patiently outside for the lunch time break. In winter he was allowed to sleep indoors curling up on the rug in front of the fire every night. In summer, he slept in a snug box in a corner of the hall. Our world fell apart when our beloved sixteen year old Mike died suddenly. Amidst all the heartbreak, funeral arrangements had to be organised and poor old Rex was temporarily forgotten. We were soon to be made aware of him in no uncertain way! As was the custom all those years ago, my lovely fair haired brother was laid out in his bedroom. The first morning after Mike's death, Rex went crazy, tearing up and down the stairs, out to the back yard and on out into the street looking for his master. Then, as if sensing Mickle's presence, he lay outside the bedroom door, uncharacteristically howling like a wolf. It was pitiful to hear. Worse was to come. In those distant days there were no such things as funeral parlours, mourning coaches and such like. A glass hearse, drawn by horses would carry the coffin with two men dressed in black sitting aloft controlling the horses with reins. As was the custom in those days, and if I can remember correctly the horses heads would be adorned with plumes, large black plumes for men and white in the case of women. After the hearse, came cabs, pulled by a single horse the leading cabs carrying family, four in each cab. The following line of cabs carried neighbours and friends. The cabs ran the full length of our street, an indication of how much loved our brother Mike was. Paddy, who had been Mike's champion over the years, shared a cab with both their boyhood friends. Just as the funeral procession was about to pull away from the kerb Rex, who was supposed to be indoors, shot out on to the street. Like a crazed animal, he shot to and fro beneath the hooves of the hearses horses causing them to rear up. Who ever said dogs were dumb animals? Did this once little scrap sense his master was leaving him for good? I think he did. All efforts to restrain and get hold of him were met with uncharacteristic snaps and snarls until finally, Paddy left the cab and lifting him gently placed him indoors and closed the door firmly. Our lovely clever and compassionate brother Mickey was leaving our street, never more to return. Even now, a thousand memories later, I can still hear his voice as he assured mum , "Ma, don't worry, I have half a crown you can borrow but you will have to give me sixpence interest when you pay it back" Finding and reading his little diary some months after his death was heartbreaking! Ah, that boy would have gone on to greater things! There it was, all written down, how much Ma owed him and, not forgetting the three shillings he had loaned his grandad to go for a drink! And, most importantly, the

34

interest he expected to accrue from these rather serious transactions!

In the weeks following our loss, poor little Rex just lay about, indifferent to all who entered our hall. He went off his food and just lumbered about with big brown sad eyes. We fussed and petted until, in time, I think he knew his master would not be returning. Rex now belonged to all of us and eventually returned to his old self. We would have him for many more years but old age was really slowing him down. He eventually became blind and lame causing our Da to make the decision to have him put down! Our father made arrangements and, in due course two men arrived in a van to take our beloved dog away. As it happened we children were all at home that day and, from the smallest to the oldest we lined up outside our hall door as our now struggling Rex was carried out. "Oh please mister, don't take our Rex" away we pleaded amidst snots and tears. We even tried to block their path as they endeavoured to take our beloved pet to the van. By now we also had the backing of the streets children as they also pleaded with the men not to take the dog away. The older of the two men returned and entered our hall door where my Da now stood. Placing the dog in his arms he informed our father, "Sorry mate, I just can't do it" In retrospect, I'm sure our Da was doing the right thing. It was cruel and selfish to want to hold onto our dog in the condition he was now in. Our childish passion and love for our dog far outweighed the right and correct procedures. My Ma was really mad at Da but, to be honest I would ask myself years later did she think as long as Rex was there so too was a part of her first born darling son? Thankfully, the decision to have him put down never arose again. It was taken out of our hands. We awoke one morning to find Rex had died peacefully in his sleep. A part of all of us died when we lost Mike all those years ago. The sensitivity that comes with old age comforts me with the thought that, if there is a Heaven, I like to think those two pals are now united.

Chapter Six
Genealogy

If I am honest, I did not have the luxury of spare time, holding down a full- time job, as well as looking after my husband and two children. Fate, Karma, call it what you will, dictated otherwise when I was required to produce an old family certificate for a project I was researching. From the moment I held it in my hands, the information it contained left me with more questions than answers! Thus, I was baptised into the world of genealogy, a passion that would consume my every waking hour for the next few years. I set out to put flesh on the bones of stories that had bridged over two hundred years, hoping in my ignorance and naivety to part the curtains of mist that had fallen silently behind the ancestors I was researching. Ah, in retrospect, I think it would have been easier to take the Pope's inside leg measurements! While I found the information on my parents and grandparents easily obtainable, beyond them the path to my past became littered with boulders of disappointments that appeared insurmountable, with no clues or illuminating lights to a past that was gone. When Mother Genealogy managed to capture and clasp me to her bosom, I was indeed hooked with no chance of escape! There are two levels at which a person functions, led by reason on one hand and emotion on the other. Between these two elements there is a no-man's land, a chasm that cannot be crossed, until a bridge appears. I reached out and found my bridge with the help of today's technology, the internet. The countless sites I found dedicated to genealogy and the experienced people on these sites who were willing not only to advise but share their knowledge, was astounding! Alas, it was not always straight forward, all of my ancestors originated from Ireland, and there were very few records pre1864. I spent my holidays trawling through musty old handwritten records, (often indecipherable), even travelling to small churches in out of the way villages, only to find them closed and overgrown with weeds. Yet, as I stood outside these places of worship, the feelings and emotions I experienced, knowing my ancestors had trodden these paths, had wed and had their children christened within the now crumbling walls, filled me with both joy and sadness. I marvelled at their faith, a faith that would force them to walk the many miles from their homes every Sunday to partake of the Mass. I would take and send away for as many as four certificates at a time, hoping against hope the name I was seeking was that of my great or great great Grandparents. Oh, the many disappointments when they were returned, but not with the people I had hoped to find, but people with the same names and birth years, but not my family! My expectancy would be dashed against the rock of despair on many occasions. On the other hand, the joy on a returning certificate being the correct one was akin to winning the pools! (Yes, it does get as serious as that.) Try as I might I could not get back any earlier than 1836. Through all my research, I discovered facts that literally made me weep, the times of the Irish Potato Famine, with the mass exodus from rural Ireland to the cities, in search of food and work. My great Grandparents were a part of this exodus, sadly arriving to find conditions even worse than those they had left behind. They ploughed a hard and lonely furrow. Theirs was a trinity of hunger, poverty and suffering, a hazardous cocktail of appalling conditions in tenement housing. This family was indeed shackled by a lead weight of despair. And yet, through this comprehensive compendium of hard and disastrous times, they managed to survive. The romantic part of me soared on learning my great Grandparents had eloped at the ages of just 17 and 19 years, once more to be dashed on learning they were both buried in pauper's graves.

I searched for years for their graves only to discover they both died in the workhouse and are buried in separate graves and separate cemeteries. This caused me great distress. Theirs was such a lovely love story, resulting in a lifetime of togetherness, through trials and tribulations. To learn they were parted in death was heart breaking. I like to think they are looking down from their celestial thrones, looking at their descendants and proud of their achievements. Looking back over my notes, the sorrow and anger fermenting inside of me propelled me towards making a better life for my children and grandchildren. While they had never passed on monetary funds or land to us, their descendants, they left us a legacy more precious than gold. I am so proud of my ancestors and the sacrifices they made. I will pass on what I have learned of them. Their story will never be consigned to the waste bin of history.

Chapter Seven
North Side

My Patchwork Quilt Were you to ask me what I did two days ago, in all honesty, I don't think I could tell you. Yet I ask myself how I have managed to dredge up events and happenings of 60 years ago. Had those memories been so bad, that they had embedded themselves in my mind never to be forgotten? Certainly not. While they might seem so to others, who had fortunately not known what it was like to live in such conditions, to me and my family (and thousands of other families) it was the norm. What had we to compare it with? I can honestly say the only bad memory I have to this day, is that of the rats which invaded our home and the homes of those living around us. My mind is like a boiling cauldron of memories waiting to boil over and spill out on to the pages, the memories coming so rapidly, I can't get them down quickly enough! Alas, if they could but come in their proper sequence, they might make better reading. Like a child, randomly plucking the petals from a flower, so I write as I greedily grasp those memories from my mind in whatever order they come. I can't explain the urge and compulsion which has come upon me to commit them to paper! Fear perhaps, that maybe a year or so from now they will have been obliterated from this old mind, like snowflakes falling on wet ground. Coming into genealogy late in life has taught me the value of diaries, records and papers, second of course to the spoken word. How many of us regret not listening to the words of older relatives of yesteryear? On the rare occasion when I have sat with my two grown up children (both living abroad) recalling events of my childhood, relating stories of not only their grandparents but also great grandparents, I have noted the polite replies of, "Really? How interesting", or "That's great mum, I am so pleased for you", on finding an all-important certificate. In my heart I know they are not really ready to become part of this wonderful imaginary patchwork quilt which, to me, represents my family. The recently added, rich colourful pieces representing the new additions, our babies, coming into a world where hopefully they will never know want or hunger. And as I travel back in time with my quilt, while some patches retain their brilliance, others lose it, the pieces becoming dull, dark and coarser, the far edge leading me to my great great grandparents and The Irish Potato Famine. In time, I hope my children will become interested in their background and add a rich vibrant colour to that patchwork quilt, the real reason perhaps for starting Dublin Recollections.

Chapter Eight
Sacks to Silks

One could tell it had been a magnificent hall door in its day, but that was a long time ago. Made of solid oak, one needed both arms to push it open, it was so heavy. It had somehow survived an era of prosperity and decadence which, according to the books I would read years later, once housed barristers, lawyers, and yes, even gentry! At first glance it looked as if wood worm had enjoyed many a feast on it, but on closer inspection this did not prove to be the case. The game of darts and rings, beloved of boys of the street, had left their mark on its once beautiful surface. Like an evil open mouth, the long gone letterbox left a gaping hole, causing the wind to rush through the wide hall like a train passing through a tunnel. More often than not it was stuffed with an old jumper by the tenant of the ground floor rooms as she muttered 'Jaysus. Sure it's like living in Siberia.' Somehow, the 'lions head' door knocker had survived, but never again would its 'roar' echo throughout the large house bringing a maid to open the door and inform the caller, 'Madam/Sir is not home today, but if you would care to leave your card?' The lions head door knocker was now rusted to the under plate and if the boys in our street had not managed to remove it, nobody could! How long, I wondered, since the door was last painted? A long time, many years ago, back to a time when the gentry occupied these once grand houses in the very heart of Dublin. The once gleaming paintwork had long since worn away down to the actual wood grain. Gone, just as the wealthy owners had fled to their country estates or back to their second homes in England. The houses had been sold

to unscrupulous absent landlords who, over the years, had turned the many rooms into individual flats, cramming as many families as they could into each house. I wondered how many years had it taken to go from superior residence to slum? These houses now constituted the infamous slums of North Dublin, my childhood home. While the odd one or two owners would make the effort to do repairs, even they, in the long run, gave up. Ah, but I reasoned in my childhood snobbery, despite the once magnificence of the door, surely the people my own tenement home once housed must have been the wealthiest in the whole street? I had arrived at this conclusion by the simple fact that our house was the only one in the street which had a tradesman's entrance! The door to this was adjacent to our hall door and consisted of a long passage leading out to our large back yard. The passage had doors on each end. I can never remember the door on the street being open, the wood withered and dead like it's long gone owners. With access to the passage from the back door in the yard, the once tradesmen's entrance became a dumping ground for all our unused or unwanted items. Relics of old prams, the wheels long gone to make 'bogies' by my brothers, broken chairs and other items banished by Ma to this glory hole with the words, 'Ah, leave it there, it may come in handy for something', somehow managed to fill the passage to capacity! With sometimes as many as six families sharing a house, the constant complaints of the (sometime one) toilet blocking up and the cold water tap in the back yard freezing over, former owners chose to ignore the complaints and look the other way! The family occupying the top flat always fared the worst.
Not only did they share the hardship and indignities of their fellow tenants, but also had to contend with rain pouring into their rooms from leaky roofs, causing wallpaper to peel away from walls and bedding to become sodden with rainwater. While many tenants referred to the rent collector as the landlord he was, in reality just an agent for the owner, collecting rents and listening to the ever constant

barrage of complaints. To be an agent, one needed a pair of strong shoulders, a skin as tough as an elephant's hide and a heart made of stone. The above mentioned door was almost flung off its hinges as the very tall, heavy figure of Mrs Chapel emerged. She stepped on to the flagged top of the four steps, one of the only four houses in the street which had steps leading up to its front door. Glancing upwards at the overcast sky, she stretched her arms straight outwards, hands gripping the black fringed shawl, ready to wrap it even more tightly around her broad shoulders against the chill of the morning air. The home- made sack 'apron' only emphasised the large belly even more, as it reached down, almost touching the top of the large black boots she always wore. One's attention was drawn to the two cut-outs in the boots, holes deliberately made to afford her some comfort from the curse of aching bunions. She looked older than her years. The once luxurious hair, now grey in parts, was pulled to the back of the head in a coil and held in place by large hairpins, as was the style. As yet, the face was unlined but looked sallow, with dark shadows under the eyes. On the rare occasions when she smiled, something of the beauty she once had been would come through. Her teeth, probably her best feature, were still perfectly even and white. One was reminded of the figurehead on the prow of a ship, but her enemies likened it to 'more like a large black bat out of hell!' The movement exposed the shabby grey jumper, strained to encase the large, pendulous breasts, an indication of the many small mouths that had suckled in their warm folds. She had actually given birth to eighteen babies in all, but lost one still born baby and two teenage girls to the dreaded tuberculosis. Large families were the norm in our street, usually ten or eleven children. To date, Mrs C held the unenviable record for having the most children. She was much feared and while she was capable of fighting any woman or man in the street, she was well respected as a 'good knocker outer'.(Meaning she would do anything legal or illegal to get the money to feed her large brood). When she could get it, she sold black market chocolate from a tray, held in place by a string slung around her neck. She even earned a few shillings selling black market cinema tickets to people who did not have the time to queue for them, or were too lazy to do so. In those far off days, one had to queue for tickets for the Sunday night cinema performances. Each person was allowed two tickets. As you can imagine, not only did Mrs Chapel join the line, but also every member of her family who was old enough to do so. She would have borrowed the money to buy these tickets. On the Sunday evening, the tickets would be sold above the face value, probably to some young fella eager to impress his mot! The money she had borrowed would be paid back and she would walk away a few shillings better off. Her most profitable business venture was purchasing large sheets of crepe paper from the wholesalers. The whole family, (now, credit where it's due!), yes, even Peter, her husband, would be roped in to cut and form 'rosettes' in the colours of the two teams due to visit and play at Croke Park. I'm told their rooms looked like a conveyor belt, with each member doing their bit. One cutting the appropriate sized strips, another forming the rosette, while yet another was busy with a paste brush gluing the whole thing into place. They would work well into the night, with even the smaller children carefully packing the finished badges into paper sacks. The whole family would endeavour to find prime pitches on match days. They stood with both teams' colours attached to large boards. As soon as these were sold, the father, doing the rounds with the paper sacks, would once again replenish the boards. Straight pins were supplied. Mrs Doyle, one of the older ladies in the street, was a tiny frail figure and in very poor health.

On the rare occasion when her husband had to go out, one of the neighbours or their children had to sit with her as she was terrified of being left on her own. God! She could talk for Ireland and, despite never leaving her rooms, she was up to date on all the street's gossip and knew everything about everyone in the street! I reluctantly sat with her one evening and the conversation turned to Mrs Chapel. While I had no problem with Mrs Doyle, I was terrified of her dog! Sure, hadn't she been a statuesque beauty in her day, her lovely face set off by a mass of thick black hair and wearing her trademark gold gipsy earrings. Sure, every fella for miles around was daft after her, she could have had the pick of the crop, yes, even moneyed fellas and she goes and ends up with that 'little runt'. The 'little runt' referred to was Mrs Chapels husband Peter, who apparently never did a day's work from the day they married! Mrs C would not hear a word said against him, proclaiming to one and all,'My poor Peter is of a delicate disposition. God love him. Sure, isn't that why he has to depend on the auld dispensary money.' While none of the streets women would dare to disagree with her, one (brave) neighbour (out of earshot) would fold her hands beneath her arms as she sniffed loudly, 'Delicate my arse! He's not very delicate when he gets between the sheets churning out babies.' Strangely, while the couple were not very popular, she because of her bullying ways, and he because of his laziness, they were both invited to every wedding and hooley going! The reason for this became apparent, as they rolled home well lubricated after such events. They would roll up the street, arms linked, singing their hearts out. Even their biggest enemies would have to concede they were the most wonderful singers. She, reaching the highest notes effortlessly, while he harmonised beautifully. They were so good that people were prepared to overlook their faults, to avail of their entertaining talents. Mrs Chapel now stood on the top step clutching the stained rent book in her hand. She did not have a clear view to the top corner of the street, from whence she knew the rent collector would appear. Clutching the railings by the side of the steps, she heaved her large frame down until she was stood on the pavement. She wiped the rust she had collected from the railings from her hand by rubbing it against the side of the shawl. She fretted and worried, furtively looking around to see if anyone else had heard the news and, like her, was waiting to catch the rent man. He would have a few houses to visit before reaching hers. All those calls to make before he reached her! She consoled herself muttering, 'Sure, Jaysus, half of them won't answer the knock on the door.' Right on time Mr Cody, the rent collector, appeared around the corner. Even if one did not recognise him by the large ledger he invariably carried, his size and clothes made him easily identifiable. A Cork man, he was six feet four in height and always wore a tweed jacket with wide grey flannel trousers, white shirt and a tie. Like many of the men who worked behind desks for Dublin City Corporation, he too always had a couple of fountain pens peeking from his breast pocket! I think they thought it impressed and indeed intimidated the slums' people, giving us the impression that they were men of letters and well educated. Sure, what would we know? Mrs C watched and waited as he entered the first house. It took him some time, so she figured out he was in luck there and had collected the rents. She was impatient and could not bear to wait while he entered the next house. Mr Cody spied the tall, unmistakable figure of Mrs C rushing towards him. While he was amazed to spot the rent book appear from beneath the folds of the shawl, he still had time to mutter under his breath, 'Sweet Jesus Mary and Joseph, here comes trouble.' 'Ah, there you are Mr. Cody, a bit chilly this morning, isn't it?' 'Well now, it's not too bad, I've seen it worse.' Pushing the rent book into his hands and smiling broadly, she loudly proclaimed for the benefit of Essie Morgan who was passing on her way to Mass, 'There's me rent and,' (with a flourish) 'a shilling off the arrears!' Mr Cody was certain now there was something afoot! No hassle getting the rent this week, but the shilling off the arrears really had him worried!

He took the book and entered the amount, at the same time deducting a shilling off the five shillings already owed. Lowering her voice, she edged closer to him as she whispered, 'Have you heard about my poor Lilly?' 'No, I haven't. Why, what's happened to her?' he asked in the Cork accent, so different to that of our Dublin drawl. 'Sure, God love her, she's only gone and got herself in the family way and she only after turning sixteen!' 'Ah, missus. Sure, she won't be the first and she won't be the last, will she now?' 'Well now, that's what I wanted to talk to you about. They are going to be married, but have no place to live. I have no room to put another body up, what with my lot!' Sure, three of them sleep over at me Ma's and the eldest fella has gone to work down in the country and our poor Mickey is in Artane. Sure, Jaysus, it's still like living in a sardine tin with me young ones!' 'Missus. Sure, I'm sorry to hear that, but I don't see how I can help you?' (Trying to edge away from her). 'Well now, sure, that's what I wanted to talk to ya about. Were you not aware Mr Cody, that auld Mr. Shields from number fifteen was taken away last Sunday, God love him. He was taken to hospital but has since been put up into the Union (the poorhouse). Sure, he's eighty if he's a day and he won't be coming home! Could you not see your way in letting my Lilly and her fella have his room?' 'Ah, I'm sorry Mrs Chapel but that room has already been 'spoken' for.' (nervously) Outraged voice:

'Spoken for! By who? I've been watching that place all week and saw no one go in or out.' 'Mr Shield's daughter has already asked for that room. The room she had in Ryder's Row was condemned and she did not want to move out of this area, so she is getting her Da's room in number fifteen. (Tentatively) 'Eh, I do have a cellar vacant over in the south side, would she be interested in that? It's clean and not bad as cellars go.' 'Are ya shagging mad or what? Sure, if she moved over there, I would not see hide or hair of her'. Snatching the rent book from his hand, she turned and made her way back to her own door, her face red with anger not just at the fact that she had paid that extra shilling, but at the thought of sixteen year old Lilly and her predicament. All the times she had warned her, 'Don't end up like me,' but that was exactly what she had done, poor cow. She

47

thought of the fine fellas she herself could have had, some with grand steady jobs, but then, how could she condemn Lilly for getting pregnant at sixteen? Had she not done just that? Now, here she was begging for a room in a tenement house, a place where she would have to share a toilet with dozens of other people and have a baby every year just like me. Again the 'hard' woman of the street pulled herself up the steps, as she clutched the railings, and on reaching the dimness of the first floor landing let the tears of disappointment fall, as she buried her face in the shawl and muttered, 'Sweet Jesus. Is that too much to ask for? All I want is a room where we can help with a few auld pieces of furniture and give her a start in life.' Eventually, Mrs Chapel's family did all marry and, while a few did live in our street, others lived in adjacent streets. Some had large families, but they never achieved their mother's quota! In the intervening years the wind of change had blown through the land. Women no longer allowed themselves to be treated as second class citizens, cowed down by state or church. While several members of the large family did well, the grandchildren went on to really achieve great things. A few opened their own businesses, with one lad reaching the very top in his chosen career. A now much older and more subdued Mrs Chapel was having the time of her life. Her family not only showered her with love, but could now afford to send her on trips abroad, mostly to religious shrines. This was what she wanted. Somewhere along the way Ma not only lost her boots and sack apron, Ma now became 'Mummy', who now wore Arnott's best. Now free of the struggle in rearing her large family, the following years were kind to her, mellowing her from the fierce lioness guarding her cubs into a pussycat.

Everyone was pleased for her. She, like all the other parents, had more than their share of worry and heartbreak bringing up the children in such overcrowded conditions. She deserved the best and, thankfully, her family made sure she got it. The very 'delicate' Peter would outlive his wife by several years.

Chapter Nine
Poor Auld Mr & Mrs Sullivan

This old mind of mine reminds me of a volcano, sometimes latent, yet at other times erupting like Mount Etna! Like lava, the memories come pouring out, hitting objects along life's way, thus evoking particular memories of events, places and times but, alas, in no particular order! Strange, how something as insignificant as a song, playing in the car as you drive along or even as background music in the supermarket, can, in one moment, cause a tiny rip in the fabric of time, allowing a glimpse into a past memory, long since forgotten. I was standing in, of all places, the unromantic aisle of toilet rolls, washing up liquid and other mundane household cleaners, when over the Tannoy came the strains of the song, 'Beguine the Beguine'. Our family would forever associate this song with our late mother's brother, Paddy. And, like a fast moving train picking up passengers at the various stations, so my memories gather, picking up the people who played a part in this simple story, that was played out in our tenement house. The players were Uncle Paddy, my granny, mammy, and finally Mr and Mrs Sullivan. It is hard to believe that the conditions, events, and happenings portrayed in Strumpet City (1907-1913) were written only about twenty odd years before the time of the following story. Of course, I can't remember that far back, but do vividly recall people still living in the cellars of the tenements, until at least the 1940s. While times were not as bad as portrayed in Strumpet City, living conditions had not improved or advanced in those twenty odd years. Looking back, I somehow felt I had witnessed the tail end of Strumpet City! I felt somehow that compared to a lot of families we were lucky, as only five families occupied the house we lived in. Each family had the front and back rooms of each floor. We lived on the ground floor, while my grandparents lived above us in what was called, 'the two pair front/back.' Mr and Mrs Sullivan lived in the cellar; we never referred to it as 'the basement', as I notice is the done thing today. The cellar consisted of two rooms, the larger of the two measuring about fourteen feet by twelve, if that. The smaller back room was really only a cupboard, and only fit for storage. In effect, Mr and Mrs Sullivan, like a lot of people in our street, ate, slept, and lived in this one room, their only light coming from a window that led out to the railed drop area. All they would see from their window would be a blank brick wall, but if they cast their eyes upwards, they would be rewarded with the sight of the bottom half of a person passing in the street above. The room was always dark because of its position, and the dim light from the constantly flickering gas mantle did not even reach the room's corners. Whenever mammy sent me down there, I always found the old man sitting directly under the gas light, his watery, red rimmed eyes peering intently into a book, while the old lady sat directly opposite, with arms folded gazing into the fire. A double bed took up one corner of the room, while an old fashioned dresser almost filled another wall. It carried an array of odd cups, dishes and pots. A recess on one side of the fireplace had wooden doors, behind which was kept their meagre rations. The two chairs, they constantly occupied in front of the small fireplace, and an old trunk made up their total belongings. I can't remember any covering on the walls, they were just very dark. The huge rats that invaded all the houses were a constant worry for them and, despite my da laying traps, it was fighting a losing battle.

We were literally overrun with them. The old couple would need to climb the small spiral stairs to reach the backyard to fetch water or use the toilet. Eventually, they were even unable to do this. Mr and Mrs Sullivan were considered unusual, as they were the only people of the Protestant faith living in our street. I hasten to add, not that their faith mattered to the neighbours. However, their reluctance to mix with others did. They only ever spoke to our family, including my granny and granddad, but that was probably because we lived in the same house. Sadly, they were without children but, most unusually, neither had any immediate family. Allow me to jump, just for a moment, from the past to the present. I believe the first church in Dublin to be turned into a restaurant/bar was St. Mary's church. It stands on the corner, opposite the old 'Maro' picture house in Mary Street. I mention this because this was the church where the old couple worshipped. Off they went, every Sunday morning, literally walking the few steps from the house towards the already chiming bells. As children, we ourselves spent most of our days playing in the small park behind the church. What we then called the 'church yard', is now known as Wolfe Tone Park. I am not sure if it was due to old age or illness, but Mrs Sullivan was a very nasty old woman. In reality, they were both now housebound and could only turn to my mother if they needed something. Despite having her own large brood to take care of, my mother, a woman of great compassion did her best for them. She did their washing, shopping, fetching the water from the back yard and bringing it down to them. Ma never failed to send one of us kids down to the cellar with a bit of dinner or soup for them. Mrs Sullivan had reached the stage where she was more or less ordering my ma about, never asking, but ordering, much to her husband's dismay! He was forever apologising for his wife's behaviour, while he, on the other hand was a lovely man, a true gentleman of the old school. Our normally placid quiet Nana had to be stopped from approaching Mrs Sullivan and telling her off for speaking to her daughter, my ma, as she did! Strangely, I can't remember Mrs Sullivan dying or even her funeral. All I can clearly remember was the sad, lonely figure of Mr Sullivan in that dark, dismal cellar room. At mammy's urging, sometimes my granddad would reluctantly venture down to have a chat with him, but he was a shy man who found it hard to converse with the well read Mr Sullivan. In effect, apart from a visit from the vicar once a month, the only face he ever saw was that of my mum. Perhaps it was fitting then, that she should be the one to find him when she took him his breakfast one morning. He had died in his sleep. I think he would have wanted it that way, rather than have strangers enter his little domain and finding him, now cold, in his long johns and long-sleeved vest. Ma went to the church at the end of our street to inform the vicar of his passing. He called and said some prayers and, as there was no living relative, he elected to arrange the funeral, as well as supplying a shroud. My brave mother! As well as helping with births in our street, she had volunteered to wash and dress the bodies of the dead after the holder of this office, Mrs Murphy, another wonderful woman, had passed away. And so, ma prepared to carry out her last act of kindness for Mr. Sullivan. only it did not turn out as simple she thought it would!

As promised, the vicar delivered the shroud which ma would describe for years afterwards as 'fit for a king'. Made of white satin, the yoke consisted of pin tucked white lace and seed pearls. A long way off from the plain brown habit with the I.H.S. we were so familiar with. And so, ma set to work in the dark cold cellar with the still flickering gas mantle casting shadows all around her. She had managed to sponge and wash the remains and was in the process of putting on the shroud when she came unstuck. It was made in such a way that the arms had to be threaded through the front and then the shroud fitted around the back and tied with ribbons to hold it in place. A tiny lady, mum was having great difficulty trying to support the body, while trying to tie the back ribbons. Gently laying him down, she went to the door and shouted upstairs for her brother. Ma: Paddy, can you come down here a minute? Paddy: What for? Ma: I want you to give me a hand to dress Mr. Sullivan, as I can't manage it on me own. Paddy: What!!! Me go down there! Not bloody likely Ma: Ah! May god forgive you; sure, you're nothing but a coward. Poor auld Mr. Sullivan can't harm you, he's dead!' After much persuasion and with hesitant footsteps, a very reluctant Paddy arrived down into the cellar. Ma: 'Now Paddy, you gently pull him up and hold him like that until I get the ribbons tied at the back'. A very nervous Paddy taking both arms, gently raised Mr Sullivan. into a sitting position.

'For Jaysus sake, will ya hurry up?' At this point, ma was behind and beneath the raised body when all hell broke loose! Amid uproar, a great weight descended on my tiny eight stone ma, trapping her beneath the body of 14 stone Mr. Sullivan.

Ma: 'Paddy, Paddy, why in God's name have you let go? Lift the body up again.' (No answer)

Ma: 'Paddy, where are ya? In the name of God, will ya answer me?'(Still no answer)

Ma: 'If ya don't get back in here and help me out, they'll be fitting you for a habit!'

Poor ma! Trapped beneath a corpse in a dark cellar and, to make matters worse, the only other adult in the house was granny and she, poor soul, was hard of hearing! Ma eventually managed to extract herself from beneath the body and went tearing up the stairs, ready to give the brave Paddy what for! 'Well! Where is he?' she asked granny. 'I don't know,' sniffed granny. 'He came charging up those stairs as though the devil himself was after him! He looked as though he'd seen a ghost and I don't mind telling you he did not look well at all,' she cried indignantly. It was a well known fact that granny would not let the sun shine on her only darling son, and it was even said that when he was a baby, she would warm his potty before he was allowed to sit on it! Still shaking and furious, ma left the house and headed straight to 'The Beamish' at the top of our street. She was annoyed enough to ignore the unwritten rules regarding women entering pubs! And there she found her (still) white faced, traumatised brother knocking back the whiskeys with the barely audible words, 'his eyes opened, his eyes opened,' coming from his lips! Despite ma explaining that this sometimes occurred when a body is jerked up, Paddy was having none of it. For a few weeks he acted like a snail on Prozac! Until the day he died, he earned many a free pint from his cronies, relating how he actually saw a dead man's eyes open.

Granny was adamant! 'Ya can't go to a protestant funeral.' 'Mother, I have to go. Sure, that means there won't be a sinner at poor auld Mr Sullivan's funeral'.

Granny and mammy rowed for several days and a compromise was reached only when mammy said she would

not attend the service, but would go to the actual funeral.
On a very wet, cold day, only ma and the vicar watched, as
Mr. Sullivan was lowered into the ground. When I first saw
the conversion of St Mary's Church to a bar restaurant, I
thought of Mr. and Mrs Sullivan and was very sad. What
would they have thought at seeing their church changed so
drastically? This, for them, was probably a place where, like
most of us, we could utter our most profound thoughts,
hopes and dreams, a place where, even for a short time,
they could find solace and peace. They were two human
beings who were once, albeit reluctantly, part of our
community and the tenements. How sad that because they
refused to mix in, they were denied the friendship, sharing
and wonderful qualities that were weaved together like a
rope, binding us all together through the poverty and hard
times. I knew they were not buried in the local church yard,
as no burials had been carried out there for years.
I often think of them and wonder where they were buried. I
never want it to be a case of they were here, gone, forgotten.
So, by my humble attempt at observations, I hope poor old
Mr. and Mrs Sullivan will be registered, even for a short
time, in someone's mind.

Chapter Ten
A Tenement Love Story - 1940's

Even dashing the short distance from the car to the chapel of rest we got soaked. "Jesus, rest her soul, even on the night she's being taken to the church the auld weather has let her down, can you believe it" I asked my sister as we clutched the umbrellas that were threatening to blow inside out any second. "Somehow I can't see any of the old neighbours coming to pay their last respects on a night like this, can you?" "Ah, I'm sure they will, they always do if they can manage it. They always turn up for the funerals of neighbours of the auld street" replied my younger sister. "Do you remember her when she was young," I asked? "She was only gorgeous" "Will you shag off outa that! For feck sake me names Marie, not Methuselah. How old do ya think I am? Sure I was only a child then, but I do remember her in later years" Smiling, she turned to ask, "Do you remember me Ma always saying I was the shakings of the bag coming so many years after you lot?" "Yes" I replied, "I also remember Ma saying you were like the banshee because you never stopped crying" "That was only on a Monday morning before we went to school when she was checking our hair for "Fellas" she sniffed. "Yea, and I remember you telling Ma if she found one you would shake your head so it would get away, Ma said you cried bad luck into the house every Monday morning" We had trouble pushing open the door to the small chapel due to the crowds packed tightly behind it. My sister gave me a look that said, see, I told ya so! The four candles, two at the top and two at the bottom of the casket flickered at the opening and closing of the door casting faces into the shadows. "Hail Mary full of grace the Lord is with thee, blessed are thou amongst women and blessed is the fruit of thy womb Jesus" intoned a voice amongst the crowd. As one, came the reply, "Holy Mary mother of God, pray for us sinners now, and at the hour of our death, amen" I furtively glanced around hoping to see and maybe even recognise a face from the past "Who's yer wan saying the rosary? I whispered. "That's Katie Murray" "Er, I don't know her" "Course ya do, well, Murray is her married name; she was one of the Fagan's from number fifty two." "What! I almost shouted, Holy mother of God! It can't be, sure that's an auld woman! She was in my class at school!" "Have ya looked in the mirror lately sniffed my sister, sure aren't we all auld ones now?" I guessed she was getting annoyed because I had reminded her of the Banshee nickname! We joined the queue of people waiting to pass the coffin to pay their last respects, my sister whispering and pointing to faces from the past and conjuring up names I had long since forgotten. I am reminded time does not stand still and mused maybe one or two of those present would be wondering who the old lady was with Marie, my sister who was very well known! Of course, it was now my white hair I consoled myself! I was glad my visit home to Dublin had coincided with the death of Jennie. Over the years, while I had forgotten many names and faces, Jeannie was someone I had never forgotten, someone I had always respected and admired even though time had dimmed the memory of most of the people present. "There's poor Joe over there" murmured my sister as she nodded in the direction of Jennie's husband, a slight grey haired, red eyed man sobbing into a white handkerchief. I was just about to tell my sister how, as teenagers we had gazed at the then blonde haired Joe worshipping him from afar but, apart from the fact he was too old for us he only had eyes for Jeannie.

I was stopped in my tracks by the auld one in front of us in the queue, "Will youse two shush, have yez no respect, talking during the rosary?" Ah missus I thought, you rightly suppressed our talking but, never our memories. I don't know what I expected to see when I looked into the casket, certainly not the tiny frail lady with short white cropped hair with a set of white rosary beads entwined between her fingers. " Oh my God Marie, were she still alive I would have passed her in the street and not recognized her " I remarked as we left the small chapel after the service. "Well, you would hardly remember her after sixty years away now, would you?" "I bet it will be a huge funeral tomorrow morning, Jeannie was very well liked and she had such a hard old life." I remarked. " Yes, I'd say they would have had to find a large venue to accommodate the reception for the expected crowd" "Surely they could not have a sit down meal for all of the people who attend the funeral" I asked. "Of course they will, if not a sit down meal it will be soup and sandwiches for everyone, we don't do it like you lot over there, I've never heard anything like it! Imagine, having to wait to be invited to a funeral!" "Marie, I have explained to you that some families want private funerals for their loved ones but do sometimes invite very close friends of the deceased" "Well, she sniffed, we do it differently here, who ever wants to attend just turns up at the cemetery and if they wish to, just carry on to the reception afterwards. It could go on all day; there could even be some guest artists there singing, a sad occasion yes, but we will get to meet all of the auld neighbours from the street from years ago" "Oh, and by the way if ya spot Joeboy Nolan pretend ya don't see him, he'll not only talk the socks off ya but he latches on to ya all day and, ya can't get rid of him" "I don't remember him so can't see myself talking to him" "Jasus, aren't you the lucky one so" replied Marie, some people call him "Toucher Nolan" "Why do they call him that when his name is Joeboy? "Well, lets just say you would be very lucky to get away from him without giving him the price of a pint or, a few cigarettes" I remark how times have changed. Chapels of rest, sit down meals, artists and bands not to mention heavenly choirs, (well almost!) For me, attending the funeral next day was an eye opener! I had lived away for some sixty years and thankfully, had not had the need to return home for a funeral. Of course I had sadly, attended many Irish funerals in England where I lived but, to date, never attended one where singers and music was the order of the day. They were usually quiet affairs with mourners passing around old photographs and reminiscing about past events and friendships with the deceased. I remembered a time when a death involved the washing and laying out by a good neighbour and a wake consisted of a few ham sandwiches and a dozen bottles of Guinness! When I mentioned this the following morning to an old neighbour he remarked with a wry smile, "Ah, yes, but back then we didn't have a pot to piss in". There were some very pretty girls living in our street way back then but, without a doubt Jennie Keough was striking, the prettiest of them all. I can't remember when I first took notice of Jennie and Joe. It was such a long time ago. I was aged about nine or ten and Jennie at that time would have been, in my eyes, "A big girl" I vividly remember coming home from school for lunch and always seeing them, she, leaning on a pillow to one side of the window sill of the ground floor room in the tenement house, while Joe sat outside wedged on the sills other half. Looking back I can only hazard a guess that she was then aged about eighteen. Jennie lived with her mother in one room of the house. Her mother, I suspect would have then been in her late fifties and in poor health. Jennie and Joe became a fixture, a constant a part of the street itself. Joe always there at lunch time and returning in the evening after work to take her out usually to the "pictures" I had never known them to frequent dance halls even in later years. They just appeared to be happy in their own company without outside distractions. We could always tell when she was going out!

The high wedge sandals would be left on the window sill to "dry" after having several coats of Blanco applied to the already scuffed surface. What a handsome pair they made, she having jet black hair while Joe's hair was almost white he was so blonde. She wore her hair in the then style of the day, the front swept up in a deep wave while the sides were swept back and held in place by two side combs, the rest falling loosely to her shoulders. She really was a very good looking young woman with sallow skin and black eyebrows winging outwards. Many of the street's young men fancied her but, she only had eyes for her Joe. I had always thought of her as tall but the passing of the years and my own growing up put paid to that theory, in time I outgrew her. As we approached our teens and became clothes and make up conscious we would avidly await their passing to the cinema, waiting and watching to see what Jeannie was wearing. We were never disappointed, Jennie would always have the latest fashion in clothes and make up and we, our eyes agog would follow their progress as they walked arm in arm down the street. Each and every one of us young girls aspired to be like her. If I am to be truthful, we also hoped that one day we too would have someone like the handsome looking Joe holding our hands! Ah! The sighs we heaved as he passed by and this, despite the fact he was much older than us! He was a really friendly chap, always passing the time of day and showing great respect to the older people of the street, everyone loved Joe. We, my then small friends and I became teenagers. In those swiftly passing years so many things changed, music, fashion as well as social history, the latter just passing over our heads. And yet, in all that time one thing never changed, the steadfast love of Jennie and Joe. It was as if time had stood still for them, the ever faithful Joe always there and Jeannie still passing up and down the street but now, still wearing the same hair style and fashion of yesteryear. We girls, who had once tried to copy her clothes and hair style deserted our icon in favour of the styles of the fifties. To us, Jennie now

61

appeared more like the women in the black and white pictures we watched in the Maro picture house. Not for us the top knot hair style and whitened wedges, wedge heeled shoes yes, and, the higher the wedge the better but, this time around, in crocodile skin no less! The passing years would see the girls of Jennie's era and years, now married and, settled down with families of their own and, yes, even younger girls. It was said she, Jeannie would never marry and leave her mother but, this theory was blown to the wind when, even years after her Ma had passed away she was still single. I, like many others wondered why they never got around to tying the proverbial knot, there was nothing standing in their way. This couple, to us then children was romance and love personified, and yes, even later a Romeo and Juliet, a Scarlet and Rhett. The phone rang and our younger sister Marie was on the line from Dublin. "Hello, how are ya, are ya sitting down?" "Oh, dear God please don't tell me you have bad news?" " Ah, no, it's lovely news. You will never guess who got married?" "I don't know, who?" "Ah, go on, have a guess" " Will you give over, I'm standing here bleeding to death having cut myself while shaving my legs and you want to play the game of twenty questions! "O.K. then, are you ready for this? It was Jennie and Joe" "No! Never!" "I'm telling you that's the God's honest truth" "I can't believe it, after all of these years, how old would they be now? " "I'm not sure about Joe but, I think Jennie would be about fifty" " Ah, that is so lovely, I'm so happy for them" "Well, everyone is, all the old neighbours turned out to watch her being wed, she had a white wedding" "I still can't help wondering why they never married years ago but, then, that's their business" I guess their compass in life had finally reached and pointed at the stage where the road ahead and the time was right for them. While their very long courtship was unusual there was no ambiguity on his part in the love he bore for her. They were two halves who became a whole and, who knows? Had they not found each other would two lives have been filled with hollowness and emptiness?

I do not know what time they had together, hopefully, a long time before Jennie's death. I had witnessed the anguish and despair on Joe's face when we paid our respects at the chapel of rest, surrounded by a scaffold of sympathy. He, Joe would follow his lost love a couple of years later. Reunited, may they both rest in peace and love.

Chapter Eleven
Dublin 1940s

As a child, I loved Sundays and not just for the lovely breakfast of black and white pudding! No, I waited for the melodious and gentle chimes ringing out from the Church of Ireland, situated at the corner of my street and Mary's Street. But soon after would come the overly loud and heavier bells of St. Ann's Church in nearby Halson Street, obliterating and smothering those of Saint Mary's. As a child, it became a worry and burden, the fact that I preferred the chimes and bells of Protestant church to those of the Catholic church my family and I attended! I pondered on this and wondered should I confess this in my weekly confession? Already, I had been indoctrinated into the fiery furnace of hell and the now defunct Limbo! What if I died? Would I never see my lovely mammy again? I weighed up this childish quandary and came to the conclusion that I would rather spend the time with my beloved mammy, brothers and sisters, and hope God would look kindly upon me when my time came! Ah, I notice I have already meandered away from the path of memories, I intended to write about. So, back to work! Sunday, and the loud bells of Saint Ann's calling the faithful to church would cause a small exodus from the tenements, and all going in the one direction. Everyone appeared to wear dark clothing back in those days, but the obligatory wearing of brightly coloured head scarves soon introduced a mini rainbow into the throng and brightened the day. I wondered if anyone noticed the elderly couple passing on the opposite side, making their way down to Saint Mary's Church? They, in passing, never raised their heads to bid a 'good morning', or even give a friendly nod. They were the only two people in our street who were of the Protestant faith. Not, I hasten to add, that this mattered. Our street always welcomed newcomers and had already offered the hand of friendship to the old couple, but sadly it was received with a closed fist. They had made it apparent they had no wish to mix with our small community. I always likened our street to a tapestry of many colours. Each stitch represented a family. It was apparent they would never become a bright stitch, but hang on the outside like an unwanted and discarded thread. Life is peopled by a cast of different people, and I realized the old couple fell within and under that umbrella. The rope that entwined the street's people would never entwine them and offer help when it was required. Despite mum having her own large family: children, her own mother and father who lived with us, we suddenly acquired two more. And, not only the shopping, but also the washing. To quote mum, 'Ah, Jesus help them. Sure, what difference is their poor auld bits of washing going make to the pile I have?' When times were good (not often), and dad was in work, they also got a meal. And so, we became acquainted in a small way with our close neighbours, after many years. I ventured into that unseen and unknown area, when I was told to take some soup down to them one day. Even at my young age, I was shocked and overwhelmed with sadness at what I encountered. Because of its situation, no natural light entered and they depended on the ever flickering gas light which did not even reach the corners of the room. A double bed with a chest at the end, a dresser with an array of odd cups and saucers, (nothing new there, eh?) and two easy chairs, made up the total contents. No wardrobe, apart from the hooks on the back of the door, to hang their clothes. I guess the chest held bed clothes and other items. Their food was stored in a cupboard, by the side of the fireplace.

The only people they would see would be the bottom half of someone walking past the railings in the street above. In effect, because they now more or less depended on our mother, the very wide chasm that had separated us all those years now slowly closed, giving us a small but better insight into this old couple. We found out Mr. Sullivan was a very well educated man of the old school, knowledgeable and always kind and courteous. He always addressed our mum with the prefix Mrs. Well, that was until she told him to call her Lou. He was an avid reader, and we never entered that room without finding him reading, his red rimmed watery eyes struggling to read beneath the inadequate gas light. He never failed to thank us, even for the smallest deed. I never see a picture of old Queen Victoria without thinking of Mrs Sullivan. Same size, same height, same shaped face and even the same hairstyle, but sadly not the same manners. She acted in a most imperious manner to the point of rudeness. And still, never a thank you to mum. Well, that was until the day she confronted mum and accused her of pinching her underwear from her washing! I should mention here our little mum was about size ten, while Mrs Sullivan was a size TENT!

Chapter Twelve
My Grandad, Master Shoemaker

I have found the pursuit of one's family through the hobby of genealogy can, like a volcano, erupt and bring forth a depth of emotions and feelings one was not aware one possessed. I have found myself having a good giggle at searching out an unknown fact about some maiden aunt, while remarking, 'Goodness me, she was a dark horse. Now that's one for the books!' How welcome were such trivial and unexpected items, much needed to break and soften the often heart breaking facts that emerged through my journey from the times of the famine in a tiny village in Wicklow, to the Dublin tenements of mine and my siblings childhood. I'm not sure what I expected to find, certainly not a bed of roses, if the tales my lovely granny had related were true, but yet, never the cold hard rock, made up of poverty, hunger and squalor, that made up a trinity I found not so holy. I recall my own mother relating how, during a strike, they had to break up and burn some of the furniture just to get some hot water ready for the midwife to deliver her first born, a boy who did not survive. I ask myself should I leave these vivid, warm, but sometimes painful memories nestled away in a corner of my mind, recalling them at will or when a couple of glasses of wine induces them, in a fit of nostalgia? I look back upon the family tree I have assembled and there, staring back up at me is the glaring omission of facts or notes beside the name of my mother's father, my grandfather. Why I ask myself did I not write anything by the side of his name, as I had done with other entries? Good heavens, he lived within my family all his life, as did his wife, my granny Julia. I was ashamed of my neglect of such a good and kind man and resolved there and then to write some of the things I remember about him in the following story, which I have named, 'Me Granda, Master Shoemaker', because I know he would have loved that. The smell of leather, wax and shoe dyes were as familiar to me as the smell of the bacon and cabbage that assailed my nostrils on a Sunday morning, coming from Mass. So too was the constant rhythmic tap, tap, of my granda at work in his workshop. I sometimes muse that this must have been the first sound we children heard as we entered the world, well, the ones who were born at home and not in the Rotunda Hospital. On reflection, one would be hard pressed to refer to my granda's place of work as a 'workshop'. In effect, it was a tiny closet measuring about 6ft x 4ft and not even wide enough to allow two people to pass each other. Were it not for the noises associated with the boot-making trade one would not have noticed the tiny closet just off the corner of a very large room in a tenement house, in what was then central Dublin. The light from the hissing gas mantle that gave a semblance of light to the larger room unfortunately did not reach the closet, and alas, there was no connection for a gas supply that would have at least given the old man the luxury of working in a light, other than that of a paraffin lamp with its tall glass globe. One would surmise that the closet had once held the 'unmentionables', such as commodes and chamber pots belonging to the rich people who had formerly occupied these slums, either that or cleaning tools. Surely even the gentry could not deem to name this tiny space a bedroom? The closet's walls were filled with hundreds of nails, each carrying not just the tools of his trade, but also the materials for shoe and boot making. Small glass jars held different sized tacks, from which a handful would be tossed out into the palm of his hand and then into his mouth. I always remember 'gagging', as I watched him do this, thinking he would surely swallow some, but he never did.

There was a window in the closet which overlooked the back yard. No attempt was ever made to clean it. Years of dust from the rasping of the leather had left a curtain of dust, held together with cobwebs, allowing no light into the tiny space. It was hard to believe the most beautiful crafted shoes and boots were turned out from 'me granda's closet', as it had now become officially known to us children. The old man knew every inch of the tiny room and, even blindfolded, could have reached out to any of the nails in the wall to select a tool or part for the shoe or boot he was working on. I would rush home from school to stand and watch as he bent over his work, only pausing to take a mouthful of tea from the ever-present large tea-stained mug. I became familiar with every tool of the trade and by the age of twelve, though lacking the strength, could in theory, make a pair of shoes. I could name every part required to make and finish off a shoe. Using the stub of a pencil, he would make out a list of his requirements and send one of us children off to the shoemaker's suppliers, Longs, not far from Capel Street bridge. We were trusted with buying all his needs with the exception of the uppers. He always chose them himself. We older children were always aware of the day a pair of shoes was completed. I think the separating of the shoemaker's last from the finished shoe, must have been one of the hardest parts of the whole process, judging from the tirade of expletives emitted from the tiny room. I'm sure he could be heard around the corner in Jervis Street! 'I'm telling youse,'my ma would say as she wagged a finger in our direction, 'Don't let me catch any of youse up them stairs till me fathers got that shoe off the last.' I had however watched once, curious to know more about this operation that caused my normally meek and mild grandfather to become the devil incarnate! A long iron rod with a hooked end was attached to the hook protruding from the shoe last in the enclosed shoe. The shoe would be held in position between his two feet, while he pulled with all his strength on the iron rod, in an effort to remove the now redundant last. The sight of the contortions and the unhealthy- looking purple hue his face adopted during this procedure was enough to send me running to hide in the small back bedroom! His wife Julia and my ma could always be found hovering on the stairs, fearing he would have a heart attack from his efforts. The staining of the welt, inserting of eyelets and laces, those final finishing ouches would be carried out before he would emerge triumphant from his cubby hole, proudly holding out his finished work. And, always, that final grand gesture. Granda would wipe an imaginary speck of dust from an already shining toecap with the sleeve of the ragged old jersey he used for work. Even as a child I would stand looking into the windows of Barry's hand- made shoe shop in Capel Street, bursting with pride when I recognized a pair of shoes or riding boots my grandfather had made, having followed their journey from start to finish. I wish I could remember what he was paid for his work, but I can't. What I do know now was that he was a pivotal part of our very existence, his contributions enabling my Ma to carry on, when my Da could not find work on the quays. As a family we were very dependent on him. On the grand occasions when he was paid for his work, he would see my ma alright, putting some notes into her hand and gently folding her fingers over them. This was followed by the now well known ritual of donning his famous brown suit for a foray to the local pubs. Ma dreaded these times. We watched as she would try and persuade her father to stay at home. 'Ah Father, why would ya want to go out on a night like this? Sure, it's only perishing outside, I'll get the jug and go up to the Beamish and get you what ya want. I'll make ya a few brawn sandwiches and boil a couple of pig's feet". While she did not begrudge her hard working father a few drinks, he apparently got carried away on these rare nights out and always managed to drink more than he should. My poor mother would stand for hours at the hall door waiting and fretting, watching out for him. Eventually, she would do what she always ended up doing, searching the different hospitals throughout the night, looking for her beloved father. And this was where she always found him, usually having broken his nose or after sustaining some other injury in a drunken fall. The strange thing was that this one outing would be the end of his drinking, and he would not touch another drop for months. When times were really hard and granda had no work he still (unknowingly) came up trumps. His beautiful brown suit was taken to John Brereton's pawn shop to help us get through yet another week. On average, it spent more time there than it did in our wardrobe. He seldom went out. As a child I always took my granda for granted. He was always there, almost like a part of the crumbling house that was our home; someone that was a part of that tiny cubby hole, because I never saw him in any other context. I now know that despite his wonderful talent, he was a very shy man who would ignore my Ma's pleadings to go and spend an hour or so talking to Mr. Sullivan, the old man who lived alone in the cellar of our house. Although he had travelled and served in the First World War, he was not as articulate as Mr. Sullivan who was a voracious reader and a very knowledgeable man. I now believe he felt intimidated by the old fellow. He paid his first and last visit one night after much cajoling from my Ma. I would be an adult before I realised what a hard working man he really was. He worked into his seventies and was basically a loner who did not mingle well outside his own family and a small close knit circle of friends. 'Why does me granda not go to Mass?', I bluntly asked my ma, as only a young child would. I notice she raised her eyebrows as she looked at my Da. 'Your granda does go to Mass, of course he does.' 'Well, I never see him there.' 'Ye'r right, I never sawn him there neither,' uttered four year old Jem. 'Well, that's because he goes to a very early Mass, while you children are still asleep.' I accepted that. When I was a lot older and my

71

granda was long since dead, I was told the following story. Granda was in the First World War and with a lot of other young Dublin men about to enter a battle the following morning. The men were eager to have confession and my granda was sent to the officer's mess to ask the catholic chaplain to come and give a general confession to the men. When he got there, he found the chaplain was in no fit state to go anywhere, having liberally availed himself of the bar in the officer's mess. While my granda was lucky enough to survive the horrors of the Somme, a lot of very young men didn't. They went to their deaths without the comfort of confession, and as a result of this the old man never entered a church again. I relate this story as it was told to me by my mother and she got it, as they say, from the horse's mouth. Granda's best friend was Michael T. They were friends from boyhood and while our grandfather went on to learn the trade of his father before him, his friend Michael knocked out a living going around with an old handcart, collecting scrap metal. In time, things started to look up for Michael and he soon had a small yard. 'Paddy, why don't ya give up the auld shoe mending and throw your hand in with me?' he suggested. I suspect granda was too scared to take the chance, having a wife and four kids to support, and the fact that he truly loved and enjoyed his work and was very proud of the shoes and boots he made. He passed on the offer. His friend, Michael, meanwhile went from strength to strength, in time tendering a bid and winning the contract to remove all the old tram tracks in and around the city. He never looked back after that. I don't know how long it took, but he eventually did become one of the richest men in Dublin. The two friends never lost touch and Mick, as my Granda called him now, came not only for the usual chat but also to be fitted for hand-made shoes. 'Are ya up there, Paddy?', he would bawl up the tenement stairs, before grabbing the banisters and pulling himself up, puffing and panting as he did so. Apparently his well deserved good fortune had not only increased his bank balance, but had also added pounds to his already rotund figure! My granda came to the door to meet him wearing his torn gansie, leather apron and leather mitten. Despite my Ma's threats of, 'I'll kill ya if I catch yez standing looking up into Mr Tulley's face', we kids always made sure we 'bumped' into him in the hall before he went up the stairs.

How could we possibly have missed such an opportunity? It goes without saying, we did not have many self-made millionaires calling to our tenement door!! He always gave us a handful of coins and always the same request to my ma: 'Is the teapot on Julia?' Ma always managed to get a few Marietta biscuits to go with his cup of tea, as not only was he granda's best friend but one of his best customers. Me Ma loved to sit with the Evening Herald and a cup of tea in the evening. Without fail she would immediately go to the death announcements, 'In case anyone I know has died.' And so it was we learned of the death of Mr Tulley. 'Ah, Holy Mother of God, it can't be,' cried my mother, as she peered through the spectacles that were held together with sticking plaster. 'What's up now?', asked my Da from the other side of the fireplace. She did not answer him, but ran to the door calling upstairs 'Father, can ya come down here quick'. The heavy tread of my granda could be heard as he made his way down our creaking wooden stairs. The salubrious address given in the announcement confirmed that it was indeed his much- loved lifelong friend, Mick Tulley. Removing a grubby handkerchief from his pocket, he wiped away the tears from eyes that were already red rimmed with old age. Had my mother given any thought to it, she would never have uttered those immortal words, 'Ah father, sure, that's one funeral ya can't miss.' Had she forgotten the famous brown suit was yet again residing in its second home, the pawn shop? With heavy heart and feet Paddy made his way back upstairs to impart the bad news to our granny, Julia. Within the next half hour, we again heard his footsteps rushing down the stairs and the door of our room was almost torn off its hinges, as it was flung open smashing against the wall, and framing a now white faced granda in its opening. 'Father, father, are ya all right, what's the matter with ya', cried ma, as she ushered him to the auld sofa by the side of the fire. 'Quick, run next door and ask Mrs. Brown if she has a drop of whiskey I could borrow. Tell her me father has taken very bad,' she ordered my older sister'. The old man finally managed to get his breath back and still ashen faced looked at his daughter and managed to whisper, 'Oh God, Mick collected his new shoes on Tuesday, and was supposed to bring the money in for them today. Sweet mother of Jesus, what am I going to do now?' Even my Ma's face blanched at this news. 'Father, I just don't know what to tell ya. Sure, we can hardly send them a bill or ask for money at a time like this.' At this point my father interjected. 'When you go to the funeral could ya not call one of the sons aside and mention it to him? I'm sure they would understand the position you're in.' At this point, ma was killed trying to catch my da's eye, because he too was unaware the best suit was in hock. 'What!' roared the old man, 'Ask for the price of a pair of shoes that is most likely in the coffin with him. Do ya not realize we were man and boy together. How could I do that?' He continued to sit there, the sword of Damocles hanging over his head, as he pondered on how to overcome this unforeseen dilemma. Me ma had yet to enlighten him to the fact he could not attend the funeral for the purpose of paying his respects and hopefully, by some miracle, getting paid for the grand pair of brogues ordered by the man, now a corpse, lying peacefully in a very expensive coffin. When he did learn he could not attend because his best suit was in the pawn shop, I think he was secretly relieved; as mentioned he was a shy man and would have really felt out of place at what he knew would be a very large funeral, attended by many of the city's dignitaries. Ma was informed she should go in his place, 'You will represent me,' said the old man. It should be mentioned here my poor ma had never been further than Dollymount in all of her life. The thought of getting a train

in Amiens Street and going to a far off place named
Balbriggan put the fear of God into her. There was no
money to pay for the train fare, until various aunties and
uncles clubbed together, so granda could be represented at
the funeral of Mick Tulley. Ma set off early on the day of the
funeral allowing time to find her way into the unknown
area. She had borrowed Auntie Bridget's best black coat and
Mrs. Brown's small black feather hat.

We would learn, on her return, that when she arrived at the
station and asked directions, he was directed to a very large
house in its own grounds some two miles away. She walked
there not having the money to pay for a cab. We waited all
day, anxious to learn how she had got on and no one more
so than me granda. It was late evening when she returned,
clutching a large brown cardboard box to her chest. 'What
kept you?', were my granda's first words to her. 'Ya had us
all so worried, we thought you had gotten yourself lost!
Anyhow, come and tell us all about it.' So, while my ma sat
sipping a longed for cup of tea, adults and children alike sat
around as she described... 'One of the biggest funerals I
have ever seen in my life, Father. I have to tell ya, the house
was so huge and posh, I was afraid to knock on the front
door. I went around and knocked at the back door and it
was opened by a woman who said she was the housekeeper.
I explained who I was and she was very kind and invited me
in. I did not make myself known to the family, as they were
entertaining some very important looking people in the
parlour. As the funeral moved off from the house, we both
peeked from behind drawn curtains as it passed. Sure, I
thought the procession of cabs was never going to come to
an end! Father, I'm sorry, I did not follow the funeral, but
sure I did not know a soul there and was not in the position
to ask for a lift!' 'Well, what did you do? What kept you so
long?' 'I sat in the kitchen with the housekeeper most of the
day. You would not believe the size of that kitchen. It was as
big as our back yard and wait until I tell youse this! They
had a huge room off the kitchen they called the pantry, and

I swear it was better stocked than the Maypole Dairy. I swear, I am not talking about pounds of butter and sugar here, but boxfulls! As for the meat, well, when the funeral party returned to the house there were platters of every meat you could mention, carried through from the kitchen to some other part of the house, probably the parlour.' 'Did you see any sign of Mrs Tulley?' asked my granda. "Yes, father I did, she came through the kitchen at one point to ask Nora, the housekeeper, to arrange for more bottles of spirits to be brought in. The housekeeper explained that I was the daughter of the shoemaker Paddy. She shook my hand and said he had spoken of you often. I said how sorry you were that you could not attend the funeral because of ill health. Well father, I had to make some excuse and I could hardly tell her you couldn't attend because your best suit was in the pawn!' We all wanted to ask the burning question, but we children did not dare to raise an issue that concerned our grandfather. We could see he was itching to ask our mother had there been any mention of the payment for the shoes. My mother decided to take the bull by the horns and put him out of his misery. 'I'm sorry father, Mrs Tulley did not make any mention of the shoes, and I was too embarrassed to mention it to any other family member. However, she told the housekeeper to give me four pounds of best butter when I was leaving.' Our mother shoved the brown cardboard box to the centre of the table. The best butter was shared out with the various relations who had contributed to our mother's rail fare. It would take longer for the old man to pay off the debts he had incurred in ordering the materials for his friend's shoes. His beloved wife, Julia, died aged seventy three and he followed her a year later, aged seventy five. I like to think the shoes and boots he lovingly made left some imprint on this earth, if only for a short time.

Chapter Thirteen
Our Mam, the Ex-Pat One!

Although not present at the time, it did not take a great stretch of the imagination to picture the scene, as described by our sister. Ah, but first a brief scenario. Our great grandparents had fled Wicklow at the time of the Famine, seeking a better life in Dublin, only to find they had jumped from the frying pan into the fire, as the old saying goes. Our great grandfather found out that shoe/boot makers were ten a penny and it was very difficult to earn a living. However, a later photo shows he managed to open a small and decrepit shop and they and their two children made their home nearby in what was then Stafford Street, a couple of hundred yards from the city's centre and O'Connell Street. Their children were William and Julia, the latter, Julia, was our grandmother. A total of five generations would eventually live in this street and from each generation the name Julia was carried through and all as a tribute to a much-loved grandmother from those who could remember her. Even after she passed on, the name Julia survived to the present day. Julia, our nana, married and had four children, one boy and three girls. Our mother Julia was one of the girls. When our mother married our father Michael, (Mick) they lived in Moore Street. Mam would later regale us with the stories of rats as big as kittens and, on reflection, why not? Life for the rats must have been akin to living in a five-star hotel, with all the food that surrounded them in the famous Moore Street Market, not to mention the nearby abattoirs. Later they would live in Parnell Street, until finally they managed to get a room in the street where she was raised, Stafford Street. The delight was doubled when the room was in the same house as her mother, Julia. The house she was born in. We were now a family of eight living in what I called one and a half rooms! A tiny 'parlour' and much smaller room which just held the table and chairs. How blessed we were to have our grandparents living in the same house. Their generosity enabled us to stay together, by allowing us to have their large 'drawing room' which we divided into extra bedrooms. My older sister would also marry and live in the street for a short time. Her two boys were born there. So, in effect, five generations of our family lived in this street. Our mother was delighted to get rooms in this street to be close to her own parents, who both lived with us until their deaths. While I remember hard and rough times, I shudder when I think what it was like for those who went before us. Sadly, we lost our oldest brother Michael at the age of sixteen. Our father was in the army and away in Italy at the time of his son's death. He was refused compassionate leave. I will not dwell on Michael's death. I have already written of it and the utter heartbreak endured by our mother at that time and, indeed, for years to come. Like thousands of others, our father returned home after the war ended. And, like many others, he could not find work, no matter how hard he tried. He did not have a trade, apart from working on the quays, loading and unloading boats. Even then he was lucky if he got a day's work. It was a bad time for our family, but I admired our father's work ethic. Every morning he would get up at all hours and, even when it was pouring with rain, he would still go out looking for work. In desperation, he was forced to leave home and go to England to find work. We were now a family of four girls and three boys. We were in our teens and out working. Looking back, I remember my wage was twenty-five shillings a week and, after six months, it was increased to thirty shillings a week. My siblings would be on a par with me.

Our mam was now looking after her aged parents. While granddad was no trouble and a great help, our grandmother was like an extra child. While back then, it was described as 'going into their second childhood', I would hazard a guess it would now come under the umbrella of dementia. She, nana, would go rambling off and our mam would spend hours looking for her. Nana would insist our mother be in bed by six o'clock and her family likewise! She, nana, would take no heed of us, when we tried to keep her safe. It was a very traumatic and worrying time for our mother, the normality of everyday events and happenings was very much shadowed by doubt and fear. Fear that nana would ramble off and have an accident, or worse get lost and not be found. Visions of yester- year, how fast they slip away, disappearing and fitting into clouds of forgetfulness! And yet, one little memory somehow managed to escape and remain with me through a tsunami of memories. Our beloved nana, a sweet and gentle lady of the old school, while taking no heed of us, would listen to her golden haired and favourite grandson, Jem. I have watched from afar when nana, thinking she was unobserved, would leave our street intending to go rambling to God knows where. And Jem, busy in a game of football, would catch sight of her and, without hesitation, leave the game and gently take her by the hand and lead her back home to safety. And the adoration, as she looked up into the face of the innocent young boy that she loved and trusted, was something to behold. Jem had no fear of the other boys making fun of him, while he made sure his beloved nana was safe. The jibes passed over his head like the proverbial water off a duck's back! I had often wondered why, that despite the love and esteem we held our nana in, she would only listen and follow our gentle Jem. When I would catch sight of him stroking her face and gently walk her home, it never failed to bring a lump to my throat. Our dad was still working away in England and sending money home to our mam every week. He would come how once or twice a year and, to our delight bring home goodies that were the unobtainable in Dublin. And yet, as young as I was, I always detected a note of despondency when it was time for his return to England. Apparently, for years, our father had wanted mam and all of the family to go and live there with him. Our mam would not hear tell of it, 'Leave me mother and father? Never!' She was adamant she was not going any place and, despite the many pleadings over the years, she stuck to her guns! Her mother or father would not be going into any 'union'. And they never did. Both died at home. Nana first, followed by our grandfather, about eighteen months later. Our father resumed his pleading and mam's new excuse was she could not leave her widowed sister, Bridget, who depended on her. Meanwhile, we had all grown up and left home. Most of us came to live in England, although one brother and sister returned to Dublin, as they could not settle in England. One younger sister was soon to be married which meant mam would have been on her own. We, the family, got together to discuss the pros and cons of mam's position. I was worried, pointing out mam would not be given a house in Dublin and would most likely be given a flat, where she would be cut off and away from all of her old neighbours and friends. Would she settle down in a new country, with new customs and ways? 'Well, we did,' one sister ventured 'and mam will, she gets on with people.' 'Yes,' I agreed, 'we did, but we were young, remember. Mam is old now and may not adapt to things and people as we did.' As a family we were tormented, as to what decision we should come to. We wanted the very best for our beloved mam, but she was worried about leaving her sister Bridget. Our sister, who had returned to Dublin having not settled down in England, encouraged our mam to move, promising she would look after Bridget. I should mention this was a great sacrifice on her part, as she already had six young daughters to look after and Bridget had odd ways about her.

However, she certainly looked after her aunt and made a great job out of a difficult situation. We owe her so much and will be forever in her debt. (A million thanks May) So, it was settled. Those of us who already lived here were so delighted our mother would be back in our midst.

Our father had a bad accident and lost a leg. The then small amount of compensation was enough to purchase a house, two doors up from me. Da suggested mam should give the furniture away and start from scratch. That almost started world-war three! 'What! Ya want me to give me mother's lovely round polished table away? She's had that years.' 'That's what I mean. It's time ya got rid of it.' 'Really, you've become very flaithulach in yer old age. The next thing you'll be telling me to get rid of me mother's beautiful glass shades, the ones with the Sacred Heart and the Blessed Virgin. Do ya know how long me mother has had those for? Sure, she was offered a fortune for them and would not part with them for love nor money.' And so, the arguments appeared to go on for ever. The trouble was mam would not throw anything away, always saying, 'that might come in handy for someone someday.' I'm sure she still had our christening robes and communion clothes packed away some place! 'Right', she said to our sister, 'we shall tell the 'ould fella we will order and arrange the transport of our goods to England, and, who knows, when we send him the bill we might add a pound, or even two?' Sadly, that plan did not come to fruition. Dad came home from England and made all the arrangements himself. On the day of removal, the whole operation turned into a farce not unlike a version of 'Mrs Brown's Boys'. Mam took it upon herself to guide the removal men down the stairs with grannie's religious shades, which stood about three feet tall. As a child, I was extremely delighted ours was the only house in the street that had a wooden spiral staircase, a spiral from street level to the top of the house, with a tiny landing that gave access to the two doors on each one. How I wished now, we had stairs like all the other houses, as I watched the precious shades go ever so slightly from side to side and this despite having about eight wool blankets wrapped around them for extra grip and protection! The poor removal men were close to heart attacks, as mam gave orders from the side lines. 'Watch ya don't catch that bedspread on any auld nails from them bannisters.' (Blessing herself) 'Me mother passed that on to me and she told me it was hand made by the wife of one of the lads who fought in the G.P.O. God bless them.' And yet, despite the banter and the neighbours all around the hall door, ready to wish good bye, I could not help wondering what her feelings really were. We were the fifth generation ready to break the chain and leave all that was familiar and much loved behind. Did she recall the many times she had scrubbed these stairs down? Was she saddened, as she passed the corner where our faithful old dog Rex had passed away? Did she recall the time our neighbour from the top of the house had discover her unconscious on the stairs covered in blood? Or our terror, when a white-faced girl from the street was sent to collect us all from George's Hill school, because mammy was very ill? Our distress when dashing breathless from school and, turning the corner, we found crowds outside of our hall door. Mam was already gone, taken to Jervis Street hospital, where she stayed for four months. I can still remember the normally scrubbed white stair steps, now covered with the stains of our mam's blood. And who could forget our landlord's contribution to house maintenance? (Titters) A coat of a wash, distemper-coloured red, red raddle. We girls who lived in the street became adept at switching when 'courting' in the tenement halls. We made sure the boy had his back to the wall as we tried to avoid getting the distemper on our coats or suits, a sure sign you would be refused a loan at the local pawn shop. We pondered about the move. Had we made the right decision? Were our reasons selfish? Did our longing to have our mother live near us, justify such a huge change for our beloved mother? The house was ready, painted and papered with all in place, just awaiting the shipment of their furniture. Surely this had to be a world away from the tenement room left behind? The outdoor toilet was a disappointment, but the large bathroom, a parlour, three bedrooms, sitting room, long hall and lovely size kitchen, more than made up for the outdoor toilet.

The big plus was the family lived all around her, apart from the brother and sister who had returned to Dublin. Her first question was, 'Where's the Church?' Mam went to Mass every morning and, while I went with her a few times until she got to know her way, she soon got talking to Sheila, a lovely young Irish lady who lived in the same area. They would meet every morning and go to Mass together. We had a few Irish families living near and about. I showed her places she would need to know. We started at the local post office and I encouraged her to go to the counter alone, while I stood nearby. I saw her talking to the clerk and it was apparent he either did not hear her or did not understand what she was saying. Again, he bent forward as she asked for, 'tree trupenny stamps.' He looked at me as if to say, 'Can you help?' I asked for the three threepenny stamps and, I suspected I saw a sigh of relief! As we left the post office my wonderful, lovely, compassionate mam declared, 'Do ya know B, that poor man should not be working there, he is stone deaf.' Our next adventure was a trip into town on the bus. There was a long queue on this very cold morning, with people flapping their hands to keep warm and stamping their feet. My mam was getting very impatient and stepped to the edge of the pavement looking for the bus that still had not come into view. Turning to me, she declared, 'I don't think this shagging bus is ever going to come'. There was complete silence from the queue, as they all looked in horror at this five-foot nothing, gentle lady using such language! Grabbing hold of her arm, I drew her to my side and whispered, 'Mam, you can't use language like that.' An indignant, red-faced mam drew herself up to her full five feet. 'What do you mean? I have not sworn, what are you talking about? All I asked was when is the shagging bus coming.' 'Mam! There you go again, you can't say that, it's swearing.' 'Well, it might be swearing here, but it's not where I come from.' And so, we encountered many such happenings along the way. Entering the butchers: 'Can ya show me that piece of pork in the window, please.' 'Certainly, ma'am.' He removes said piece of meat and shows it to mam. 'Can ya turn it to the other side please.' Butcher turns it. 'How much is that please.' 'That will be ten shillings and sixpence ma'am.' 'What! There's only the makings of a decent sandwich in that! Are ya mad? I'd get that in Moore Street for five shillings!' The butcher is looked in astonishment at this crazy woman who has dared to enter his shop and complain about the price. I hurry Mam out of the shop and, when out of sight of the butchers, I laugh until I almost choke! 'Mam, let's go home and get a nice cup of tea, you have a lot to learn.'

Chapter Fourteen
Phoenix Park

It is strange when reflecting and looking back on one's childhood, how well one remembers the simple things that gave us so much pleasure. Halcyon summer days walking to the Phoenix Park with a 'borrowed' baby, if the family did not have one of their own. What a sight we must have made! Even the prams left a lot to be desired, having been passed down through the family; some, their buckled wheels determined to go their own way, as we endeavoured to push them in a straight line. Yet, even these were better than the homemade hand-carts, made from a couple of old orange boxes with two long, homemade handles, nailed to the sides to push them! An old cushion or pillow would be placed in the box for the child's comfort. As many as eight of us would take part in this 'excursion', with our assortment of old prams and box-carts blocking up the whole footpath, much to the annoyance of the auld ones making their way to Mass in one of the several churches along the Liffey. We went well prepared for our day out with bottles of water, a jam sandwich and, if we were very lucky, a bag of broken biscuits from Mrs O'Toole's corner shop. Not for these babies the fancy banana shaped feeding bottles on show in the windows of Mr Timothy's chemist! Why spend precious coppers on those, when an empty Chef's sauce bottle, filled with milk, would serve the same purpose? We walked along the path opposite, as the one nearest the water was too narrow to accommodate our motley crew. Sometimes a few of the street's boys would tag along, but thankfully, that did not happen too often! I certainly never wanted to see that horrible Billy Allen. All he ever wanted to do was play Cowboys and Indians, his small blocky frame always running ahead, as he smacked his bottom crying, 'U-a U-a all the gang.' We would listen out, hoping to hear the deafening warning hooter of a Guinness barge, as it approached one of the many bridges. How we hoped we would not be 'between bridges', or it would involve a mad dash with our unreliable transport to make it to the bridge in time to watch the barge pass under it. Somehow, we always made it, minus a wheel or two, and oh, our joy, as we stationed ourselves in the centre of the bridge, watching and waiting as the barge came chugging up the river towards our vantage spot. None of us were tall enough to see over the bridge's parapet, so dozens of little toes wedged themselves between the balustrades and small hands gripped the hard, cold stoned top of the bridge, as we hauled ourselves up to rest our top halves on its wide ledge. Holding our breaths, we would wait for the moment, silent, until we saw one of the bargees start to lower the huge funnel, thus enabling the barge to pass under the bridge. This was the sign to cheer, scream and shout in anticipation of the moment we were waiting for! Then it came, the huge cloud of steam enveloping us in its mist, until just for a few moments, we were lost from each other. How I have relived these moments, when one was thrown into a white world, smelling that peculiar smell of steam, with only the shrill screams and giggles of my small playmates assuring me I was not, thankfully, on my own. And yet, another mad dash across the road to the opposite side of the bridge, and just in time to watch the barge emerge from its dark cavern! While the Guinness boats would give us children so much pleasure, their contents would bring disruption and sadness to many, as I would learn some years later. We would continue our journey to the park still discussing the 'terrifying' experience we had just been through! When we reached Collins Army barracks near Benburb Street, we always stopped to admire the large cannon placed in the centre of the lawn.

We waited to hear the same old story from Chrissie Mac, as she related how, 'Me granda told me that this was the gun they used to run the Tans out of Ireland.' Behind her back Esther mouthed, 'dirty little liar' and then, to her face, 'Sure, for Ja--s sake, that auld thing is so rusted it hasn't been fired since Noah built his auld ark.' Chrissie, red faced and tossing her glorious black curls: 'And what would you know? Sure, wasn't my granda there during the troubles so he should know what he's talking about!' Esther: 'Your granda my arse, aren't ya forgetting I was the one who won the holy picture at school for me knowledge of Irish History?' 'Yeah, and we all know ya would never have won it, only Mary Malloy was off sick with them auld mumps. Sure, she's miles better than you at the Irish history, clever clogs.' The pointless childish repetition only came to an end when it was suggested that we should eat now as 'had we not travelled and pushed these prams for miles?' (one mile). Nothing tasted better than those jam sandwiches and bottles of water. The babies were given their milk from the glass Chef bottles and some broken biscuits. We would have eaten our 'rations' before reaching the park, but unperturbed would carry on spending the day rolling down grassy hillocks and having competitions to see which one of us could race up the steps of Lord Gough's monument in the fastest time. Alas for the poor ducks in the pond, we never had a crumb left to feed them!

Chapter Fifteen
The Blue Shawl

Clutching my mammy's hand, we left our home passing the five houses before reaching the pub on the corner and turning into Parnell Street. I think the pub was called McCoy's, but was known to everyone as, 'The Beamish'. Secretly, and behind mammy's back, I stuck my tongue out at the building as we passed. The previous week daddy had promised Mammy he would take us all out to Dollymount, a rare visit to the seaside. Mammy had the sandwiches all packed, as well as an array of mismatched cups, the teapot, milk and sugar. In fact, everything required to keep her large family going on their day out. On that glorious sunny day, we had waited and waited until losing patience. Mammy had dispatched my brother to 'The Beamish' to see what was keeping daddy. 'Tell your mammy I will not be long, tell her to go on out on the bus and I will follow and catch up with you.' Poor mammy collected her large brood and made her was to O'Connell St where we caught the bus out to Dollymount. What a sight we must have made with our towels, and an assortment of shopping bags with teapot and cups peeking from the tops! Alighting from the bus, we walked along the long road leading to the beach. We passed the lady who sold boiling water for making tea. Even standing yards away, the heat from the fire under the very large container holding the water could be felt making our already sun kissed faces even redder. For a deposit, one could even 'hire' the teapot with the water, but supplying your own loose tea, no teabags in those days! Our first job, on arriving, was to collect enough kindling to make a fire ready for our tea later in the day. We children undressed, the girls young enough just to wear our knickers, as we did not possess bathing costumes. How we loved splashing in and out of the water, trying to outrun yet another large wave, as it headed inwards toward the beach. Mammy's cries of, 'Don't go out too far, or hold the hands of the younger ones', went unheeded; we were too busy enjoying our rare treat out. Later, the boys would get the fire started, amidst much puffing and blowing and mammy made the tea when the water finally boiled. Nothing tasted as good as those sandwiches, despite the grains of sand that had somehow found their way between the thick slices! From our low vantage point on the beach, her eyes would constantly turn to the upper road watching for signs of daddy's arrival, but daddy never came. Thus, my childish reason for sticking my tongue out, as we passed 'The Beamish' on our way to Moore Street. We passed the small drapers shop called 'Kenny's', where Nana had bought my older sister a pair of button-up-boots that reached half way up her legs, and I cried because she had not bought me a pair. They had lots of little hooks and eyelets and very long laces that had to be wrapped around each one, before being tied in a neat bow, when the top was finally reached. I knew all these little shops like the back of my hand. We passed the next street to ours, which was Jervis Street. At the far end, divided by Mary Street, was Jervis Street Hospital, where we would go for attention for minor to major illnesses. Now, we were passing Nellie Hoban's small shop which only sold vegetables. This was where my mammy shopped, instructing us to, 'Go round to Mrs Hoban's and fetch a stone of potatoes. Make sure they are King Edwards and big ones, and a Savoy cabbage and feel it and make sure it's got a good firm heart.' On past the large grey stone house, with the large flight of steps leading to its front door. This was known to us children as 'The Old Maids Home'. I can never recall seeing anyone go in or out of this place. When I was older, I was informed it was a retirement home for 'genteel ladies of the Protestant faith.' Almost next to the home, and many years later, came 'Peat's', an electrical shop, where we would get our very first television set. I was at my happiest clutching mammy's hand and going shopping. I could not help noticing the gaping buttonholes on mammy's dress. Oh God, please don't let my mammy get too fat. If I got into a fight in the street, sure wouldn't all the young ones (little girls) be shouting, 'Na na na na na, your mammy has a big fat belly', and then I would have to give them a slap and probably get into trouble with the nuns at school! We were now outside of Mrs Crowley's second-hand shop, directly opposite Noyek's Wood Merchants. (In 1972 Noyek's would become the scene of a tragic fire in which eight people lost their lives. R.I.P.). I knew we would enter, as mammy loved going in there. How can I now describe Mrs Crowley's shop, compared to the second-hand stalls of Coles Lane, with their mountains of clothes piled high in no order? Think Harrods versus Woolworths, and there you have it! The 'cream' of second-hand shops! A small shop, Mrs Crowley washed and starched everything before placing them in their respective places on tables and shelves around the shop: doilies, christening robes, baby gowns and binders, as well as beautiful quilts and tablecloths. 'There you are, how are ya?', a Dublin greeting, she called out to mammy, as we entered the shop. 'Ah, sure, I'm grand thanks. I just popped in to see if you had got anything nice in, since I was in last time.' replied mammy. 'As a matter of fact, I did get something in that I thought you might be interested in and put it to one side until you came by.' Bending, and reaching under the counter, she straightened up and in her hand was a shawl of pale blue, as delicate and intricate as a spider's web. Soft and silky, with long silk fringes falling from its four sides, it looked as though it would have passed through a wedding band! Mammy loved it on sight, and without hesitation paid a deposit to secure it, promising Mrs Crowley she would come in the following week to pay off the balance. 'Oh mammy, it's gorgeous. Are you going to put it on Nana's round polished table?' I asked as we left the shop. 'Maybe, we'll see.' she replied, a smile on her face. On we went, stopping to gaze into the window of Stanley's Dairy and Cake Shop. We looked in at the display of fresh cream cakes, cream buns, flaky cones, the fresh cream oozing from their centres, alongside the sugared doughnuts, crispy on the outside, but mouth-watering fluffy on the inside. I never think of Stanley's shop, but am reminded of Mondays and washday. We always knew it would be a fry up from Sunday's leftover mashed potatoes and cabbage, as mammy had mountains of washing to do. On arriving home from school, we would find her in the back yard, up to her elbows in soap suds, as she rubbed the clothes against the scrubbing board in the old tin bath. Flushed and hot, she would send one of us down to Stanley's with a jug for a pint of buttermilk. On our return, she would place it to her mouth and greedily drink until it was all gone. She maintained there was nothing like buttermilk for 'cooling you off.' Still, we carried on walking down Parnell Street, until we came to Stein's Pork Butchers where mammy always bought her black and white pudding, half a pound of brawn for Saturday night's sandwiches and of course, a couple of pigs feet/trotters for da. Stein's was, without doubt, the cleanest shop I had ever been in. Its large window boasted silver trays, full of an assortment of links of shiny skinned sausages: pork and beef, thick ones and thin ones; rings of pudding, lean or fatty black ones, and the delicious fine textured white. Mammy said no one shop produced pudding or sausages like Stein's and I agreed with her. 'Of course,' she told me, 'They were made to a secret recipe!' 'What's the secret recipe?' I asked. 'Ah, sure, if I knew that wouldn't I be a millionaire. It has been handed down from one generation of the family to the next, and when they all die out the secret will die with them.' 'What's a generation mean, mammy?' 'Ah, whist, (quiet) and go on into the shop."

The four people behind the counter wore spotless white coats, and after mammy collected her messages (shopping), the nice man behind the counter used his sharp knife, and cutting a slice off a ring of white pudding handed it to me. I loved Sunday mornings, all week we would have porridge for breakfast, but on Sunday the lovely smell of the pudding and sausages frying would have us flying down the stairs ready to tuck in. If you went to early Mass, from every house one passed would come the same lovely smell. A late Mass and one's nostrils would be assailed with the smell of cabbage and bacon, bubbling away for Sunday dinner. Finally, we reached Moore Street, but that's a recollection for another day. Some months later...Returning from school, we turned the corner into our street and I felt sick, as we spotted our neighbour from the upstairs rooms anxiously looking this way and that, until finally, she caught sight of us. Stepping even further out on to the footpath, she beckoned for us to come quickly. It was like history repeating itself. Had not the neighbours come to fetch us all home from school, when mammy had almost died and had to go into hospital for a very long time? Then I saw the smile on her face. Surely mammy could not be sick or she would not be smiling? She bundled us all hurriedly into the hall of our tenement house and up the stairs. What was that strange smell? I would later find out it was the smell of Dettol disinfectant. Ma always used the cheaper Jeyes Fluid, for scrubbing and cleaning. Ushering us into the room, we found our mammy sat up in bed in a lovely white nightdress, and in her arms a blue bundle. I recognised the shawl as the one she had bought from Mrs Crowley's second-hand shop. Beckoning us to gather round and come closer, she gently pulled the shawl back to reveal a little puckered up face, with a head of black hair. The latest addition to our family after five years! She was the most beautiful baby I had ever seen, the tiny rosebud mouth opening just like the tiny birds I had seen in my picture books. 'Oh mammy, she is gorgeous, can I hold her?' asked my older sister. Our brothers did not share our enthusiasm as they cried, 'Ah no, not another girl! Sure, she won't be able to climb or play football!' I was in my element, at last. I would have a pram to push, with our very own baby, no more going to ask our neighbours, 'please can I push your pram and baby?' For the rest of my life, I would forever associate the smell of Dettol with 'new babies'.

Bridie 6 months
pregnant with Ken

Bridie aged 7

Bridie, Jem, Julia, Louie & May

Bridie & second husband
Aidan

Back row Micheal, Paddy, Jem
Front Row, May, Monica, Bridie
& Louie

Kellogg's Corn Crackers Women's football
team. Bridie goal keeper back row

The Golden Girls: May, Louie & Bridie

Chapter Sixteen
Sure, *That Auld Saint Anthony is No Good*

How I loved the summer evenings, when we could play outside in the street, the boys usually running up and down with the rim of an old bicycle wheel and a stick which they used to 'drive' the wheel. We girls would play ball or 'piccie', using an old shoe polish tin to hop from one chalked bed (drawn on the ground) to another. I heard my mother's voice calling, even above the squeals of delight of the playing children. I pretended not to hear her. It came again, but louder this time. 'Bridget, that's the last time I'm calling you, if you don't come now I'll get Patrick to come out to you.' I hurried over to our front door. 'Ah, mammy, I can't come now, we're playing relieveo and it's my turn to be on.' 'You'll be 'on' alright, if you don't do as I tell you. Now come in and collect your school bag and clean clothes. You're going home with Auntie Bridget tonight.' 'Ah, mammy, I went home with her last night. It's not my turn, it's J's turn to go.' 'I don't care whose turn it is to go. I'm telling you to go and whist (quiet), keep your voice down, she's just inside the door and she'll hear you.' I reluctantly entered the house to gather my things together, ready to go directly to school the following morning. As stated in an earlier story, we children took turns in going home with Auntie Bridget every night, as mammy said she got lonely, as her husband was away in the war. Auntie Bridget and Uncle John did not have children of their own. I passed my sister J on the stairs and it was obvious, by the smirk on her face, she had overheard the conversation regarding my going home with Auntie Bridget. I was really bulling (annoyed), and could not resist giving her a good poke on the arm! 'Are you ready, Alana?' (Term of endearment for a child), called Auntie as she put her coat on and threaded her arms through the handles of the ever present shopping bag. Bidding goodnight to my mother, we left the house heading for her home in Hardwick Street. Oh God, I thought, I hope we don't meet any of the auld ones (old women) that she knows, sure wasn't she bound to stop and talk to each and every one of them and it would take us ages to get to her place! I could smell the fish and chips, even before we reached Benny's chippy in Parnell Street, and wondered would she stop to buy us a bag of chips. As if reading my mind she remarked, 'Sure there's no point in getting a one and one (one fish and one bag of chips) now, sure they'd be stone cold before we get home to my place. Let's wait and get them from the chippy round the corner from near me. I have a lovely crusty loaf in my bag and some real butter at home, we'll have a grand supper.' That made me feel a little better about going home with her and my game of relieveo was soon forgotten! I linked her arm as we walked along, hoping against hope she would not call into Dominic Street church to 'say a few prayers', as the previous week hadn't that cross auld Father Riley caught me and Sheila pretending to hear each other's 'confession' in the confessional boxes, and only run us out of the church! As usual, she did call in to light a candle and say some prayers; I was in luck, as we did not see hide nor hair of him! A deeply religious woman (despite her love of harmless gossip) she had a great devotion to Saint Anthony and never failed to call in and visit the shrine in Temple Street, almost opposite to where she lived. How well I remember my first visit to the shrine, as if it was yesterday.

We walked down the little laneway, to the right of the main hospital, past the door for accidents and through a door almost opposite, which led to a small hallway. The hallway led out to a lovely well laid out walled in garden, filled with flowers, bushes and trees, a peaceful place where it felt safe, and somehow cut off from the outside world. I likened it to the secret garden I read of in my library books. I had never been in such a place before. While we had no gardens in our tenement houses, I had of course visited the Phoenix Park, along with the other children of the street, yet, somehow this was different. I was not overwhelmed here in this place, as one was with the vastness of the latter. We turned right along a narrow path and towards what looked like a tiny chapel. On entering, I was surprised to find not a church, but a small room with an altar, holding a life-sized statue of the saint. The three rows of candle holders were already full, their flickering flames casting shadows high up to the vaulted ceiling, within this small space. There were four pews with red velvet kneelers and space for two people on each pew, which filled the back wall. We knelt and prayed in the silence. Well, Auntie Bridget prayed, I was too busy thinking of the fish and chip supper we were going to enjoy later on! The door opened and an auld fella (old man) entered. He knelt and prayed for a short time and then went to a small table in the corner, I had not noticed before. I watched as, taking a small sheet of paper and a pencil from a basket, he wrote something on the paper before placing it in the small basket on the alter, adding to the many others that were there. 'What's he doing,' I asked. 'He's writing a petition, 'replied my auntie. 'What's a petition?' 'Well, er, it's a request. A kind of plea, asking the saint for something he wants badly.' 'Like what?' 'It could be anything. He may have lost something that he wants to find, or he could be praying for someone that's sick. Ah, sure, it could be for anything.' 'Well then, how do they post them to Saint Anthony?' I asked, thinking of that auld postman of ours who would not even go up a flight of stairs to deliver, but stood in the hall shouting out the name, until the person came all the way down to collect the letter. What were the chances of getting these (what had she called them) to heaven? 'Well, go on then, tell me how they get to heaven?' 'When the basket is full of petitions, they are burned before the altar of Saint Anthony, and don't you worry, he gets them and knows what each person is praying and asking for.' 'Can a person ask for anything?' 'Yes, within reason.' 'And could I ask for...' was as far as I got. 'That's enough,' cried Auntie Bridget. 'Now let me get on with my prayers.' 'Could I just ask one more question? Can I write out a petition?' (I had learned a new word!) 'Yes, yes. Why don't you ask for Daddy and Uncle John to come home safely from the war?' I felt my face go red with guilt, that wasn't exactly what I had in mind! This indeed was fabulous news to these young ears! My eyes lit up; the possibilities were endless. Why had nobody told me of this before? Tiptoeing to the small table in the corner I took several sheets of paper and, wetting the small stub of pencil between my lips, proceeded to ask the good saint for the following: 'Could you please teach me how to turn the heel of that sock in sewing class, as I'm always getting into trouble with Sister Margaret Mary? If you (cause you're a man) can't teach me to turn the heel, could you please see that I have chicken pox in the morning, so I don't have to go to school? (Thinks) On second thoughts, I think I'll make that measles, sure didn't Mary Muldoon just tell us in school last week about her aunt who had to wear a veil for the rest of her life, after getting terrible scabs on her face from the auld chicken pox! I hate being the small fat girl with the gym slip bursting at the seams at school. Could you please make me smaller? Hang on Saint Anthony, I don't mean smaller in height (Oh God, how do I spell that word? Deat? Diet? (Better not ask Auntie Bridget, sure then she would know what I was asking for.) Well, if you would just make my clothes fit me better, sure that would be grand! Now, I don't want to be greedy, but I wonder if you could change my nose, and let me have a lovely little upturned one like my sister Julia and lovely tumbling curls like my sister May?

Oh, I almost forgot. Could you bring Dady and Uncle John home safely from the war. 'In the name of the Lord God, are you writing a book?' called out Auntie Bridget, causing me to hastily fold my papers and place them with the others on the alter. We left this beautiful place and made our way to the 'chippy', where Aunty Bridget threw caution to the wind and bought us a one and one each! We went to her place and enjoyed our supper with the lovely crusty bread and the real butter! The following morning saw me rush to the small mirror Uncle John used for shaving. I examined my face from every angle, but not a spot or blemish in sight. I consoled myself, thinking surely, they would appear before I got to school? I could not see if my plump body had diminished overnight, due to the lack of a full-length mirror. On my way to school, I peered at my reflection in every shop window that I passed, hoping that the good Saint Anthony had by now received my urgent petition, but alas I still had to attend school and the dreaded sewing class that day. 'I don't know what's got into you Bridget, sure you're getting so vain. Every time I look at you, you're looking into Nana's full-length mirror,' said my sister of the upturned nose. I thought of how full the basket of petitions had been before I placed mine, and convinced myself Saint Anthony was very busy sorting that lot out before he reached mine. Give him time! And so, I waited and waited and, in the end, gave up hope of ever having tumbling curls and a pretty upturned nose. No, sure, that auld Saint Anthony was no good! Sniffing loudly and tossing my long plaits, I made up my mind I wouldn't be writing to that auld fella ever again! But wait a minute, had I not heard Nana mention something about a Saint Jude, patron saint of lost causes? Er, now, where in Dublin was there a shrine to Saint Jude?

Chapter Seventeen
The Holy Grail

A maze of memories, trapped in a labyrinth of sadness and loss, finding no escape from the memory of a loved one just lost. How heavy the heart feels, I lie awake some nights as sleep evades me. Unbidden, many memories come to the fore, some delightful and welcome while others, I try hard to suppress and consign to the waste bin of amnesia. I have no wish to remember happenings that will awaken old wounds and sorrowful memories that have lain dormant for so many years. Yet, how can one escape the unpalatable ? If one could just pull a plug and just delete memories, leave them to gather dust in some unknown secret place never to be discovered, Ah!, if only? And yet, I ask myself, will the relating and telling of these recollections somehow ease the geyser of pain and grief that overwhelmed our family way back then? I ask myself, do memories shape us just as much as past and actual events? Passing funerals were almost a daily occurrence in the tenement street of my youth. The hearse carrying the coffin would be viewed by us children running along the footpath as we counted the amount of glass shades atop of the coffin, We children had come the conclusion the more shades the more popular and loved the deceased was. Strangely I can never remember fresh flowers, no, always glass shades with waxed or delph flowers beneath the glass domes. And, certainly no fancy funeral parlours or huge floral displays. The simple fact was people just could not afford luxurious displays, a dignified and quiet burial was the order of the day. Those who could not afford the cost of a funeral saw their loved ones buried in a pauper's grave further adding to the pain and suffering they were going through. Not for one moment do I suggest our loss was worse than anyone else's, oh no. While our parents had sympathized and offered condolences to other in their loss, they had never (apart from a newborn and first baby) had the grim reaper call to take an adult or older child. The only thing that tore us children off of the street, and away from our outdoor games, was the end of summer and the arrival of winter. Playing cards for buttons, underneath the old gas lamp outside our hall door, was a favourite pastime, until we spied the old lamplighter coming around the corner to increase the lamp-posts glimmer to a warm glow. A small man who wore a cap that was two sizes too large and bearing the city's logo. This was the only indication that he worked for the 'Corporation'. We children would jump to one side to give him access to brighten the lamp with a special key. A man full of his own importance, he loved to show his authority by trying to impress us children. 'I hope yez bowsies haven't been interfering with me lamp?' 'No mister, we haven't touched it.' 'Yeah, well make sure ya don't or I'll have the polis on the lot of ya.' As soon as he turned the corner, we were back to our beloved game of cards, but left wondering why he always said, 'polis', rather than 'police'. My own Nana also said 'polis'. We had now to find an alternative to playing cards under the lamp post, as it was far too cold. We tried Moran's hall, but Mrs Moran soon shifted us with shouts of, 'Go and play in yer are own halls, I can't hear me ears for yez.' We soon found a nice spot in the hall of Mrs Downey and, to top it off, Sheila, one of the card players, arrived with a few red votive candles, and I swear one of those was straight off her Ma's altar, as it was still warm with the wick, well burnt down. Ah, sure, weren't we grand, in out of the cold and a few candles that enabled us to continue playing! And then we heard it, screams like we had never heard before, unnatural and chilling, sounding just like Mrs Nolan's dog when it was run over by a car and killed.

103

A boy's voice shouting, 'ruggy up, ruggy up,' an indication there was trouble or a row happening in the street. Forgetting our card game, we rushed out into the street and were met with the sight of a large crowd outside my own hall door two doors up. I panicked, thinking the house was on fire, but yet could see no smoke. I now realized the screams were coming from within our house, and I was horrified to recognize my own mammy's voice. I tried to push through the crowd to reach her, just as yet another woman joined those already there. Turning to the woman close to her she asked, 'What's wrong, what's going on?' 'Ah' she replied, 'young Michael H. has just died and him only sixteen years of age.' I stopped, unable to go any further and thinking, no, this auld one has got it wrong, it can't be our Michael, not Michael our brother? Two of the street's women held me back and would not let me enter the house to see my mammy. They handed me over to two older girls telling them to take me for a long walk and, 'don't bring her back for an hour or so, I think, or, at least felt it was the longest walk I ever made, walking away yet still hearing my mammy's anguished screams. Despite my pleadings of, 'I want to go home to my mammy, please take me home to my mammy,' they stuck to the orders given by the older women, and did not take me home until two hours later. We later heard the story of what had happened. Michael, my brother, had an appointment that evening with the doctor whose surgery was situated in Halson Street. Of course, no phones back then, our mother had decided, as it was such a bad night, she would not risk taking her darling boy out. She had gone to cancel the appointment, leaving our Nana looking after Michael who was in bed. Michael took a bad turn and our Nana sent a neighbour chasing after our mother to get her back home. Mammy arrived home breathless, having run all of the way. She dashed into the bedroom, just in time to see her boy turn to look at her and hold out his hand towards her. Just two steps to take, but even that last holding of hands was denied her. He closed his eyes and was gone before she reached his bedside. We returned to a full house of neighbours, surrounding our mother who was sat in a chair unable to even stand up. The heart wrenching sobs and heaving shoulders was unbearable to watch. The rawness of such pain would stick, like Velcro, in my memories for years. A heart, filled with so much love for this boy, her eldest son, her golden boy, was shattered beyond repair. Already having lost her first child shortly after birth, Michael was next to arrive. I had, over the years, heard conflicting reports. He was born with a curved spine and, yet another version, how as a baby, a small girl had tried to lift him from his pram and dropped him, thus causing this deformity. I am inclined to believe the first version, that he was born this way. We also learned mum was told by doctors, Michael would not live beyond the age of fourteen years, as the older he grew, the spine would become more curved, and in effect damage the heart. Whatever the truth, it would soon become apparent as he grew up that while he was not born with a perfect body, he was blessed in so many other ways. People gravitated to his winning ways and not just out of sympathy. Yet, his best asset was his intelligence, nothing fazed him, he would read a lot and retain, without bother, everything he had read, soaking up his favourite Irish history and other subjects as quickly as a sponge soaked up water. He passed every exam that was set before him, even gaining a place at college which was never taken up, because our family was unable to meet the cost of books and other items. The depth of our mother's love for this child, her broken boy, knew no bounds. She absolutely adored him, as did our grandparents who lived with us. To us, his brothers and sisters, he was just our Michael. We never saw him in a different light, even pointing out to our mammy it was not fair! Why did he get those lovely tubs of malt and a special type of emulsion and we didn't? And always came the same reply, 'Michael is delicate, he is not strong like you.' If a stranger made a derogatory remark to or about him, his knight in shining armour, his younger brother, Paddy, soon sorted them out, as did his friends.

When older, I wondered did our mother live in constant fear and dread, recalling the prognosis of the doctor all of those years ago, that Michael would not live beyond the age of fourteen? And, when he passed the age of fifteen and then miraculously sixteen, did our mother think her prayers had been answered? A deeply devout lady, did she in desperation wonder why her prayers were not answered? Our father was serving in Italy then and could not get compassionate leave. Trapped in a prism of grief and trauma, we truly thought our beloved mother would die of a broken heart. It did not help that Michael's dog Rex lay outside of the room where Michael was laid out, uncharacteristically howling like a wolf and refusing to eat. All attempts to remove Rex were met with snapping and snarls, a far cry from his natural gentle behaviour. This would continue until the hearse arrived to take his master away, and even then he was snapping at the hooves of the hearses horses, as they pulled away from the house, trying to prevent them leaving. Paddy left his cab to grab him and lock him in the hall, so the funeral could proceed. Poor Rex would not eat for days and it took some weeks before he returned to the dog we loved. And, even though I was young, I could recognize the sadness in our Nana's eyes, as she saw the pain her beloved daughter was going through. Our Nana, trying to help in her own way, was chastised by mum for endeavouring to remove Michael's jacket from behind the door, where it still hung, both lapels almost covered by the small emblems and badges he delighted in collecting. So many reminders: his books, drawings and the small purse he kept for his winnings from playing 'housey, housey'. It would be much later when we found his well hidden diary with entries such as, 'Lent me grandad 1/6 to go for a pint until he gets paid, I expect to get six pence interest for this.' It would take a long time for things to go back to some kind of normality, if one could call it that. Our

106

mother cut a sad and lonely figure despite the support of our grandparents and her sisters. While death was not unknown to us, it had not yet reached out it's tentacles to grasp and take a loved one away in our family. The deaths we had witnessed in our street were usually those of old people, but, even then, to the innocent eyes of us children, a man or woman aged about forty would be considered old! We, naturally, as children, were divorced from and, yes, devoid of, the pains death showered on our non- relatives. A shroud of sadness clung over our rooms, giving us cause to be quiet and not upset our Mam any further. We asked Nana, 'When will Mam be better, she never laughs anymore?' I spent a lot of time in my grandparent's room above ours. I could not bear to see the sorrow in Mam's face telling Nana, 'I want my mammy back.' 'Hush alana, your mammy's heart is scalded now, but with the help of God it will heal.' Our mother, was now looking after her now seven children, her aged parents, and still helping out the lonely old Mr. Sullivan, who lived below us in the cellar. Our Dad was still serving abroad and, having been denied compassionate leave, had apparently gone on the biggest bender of his life on learning of his son's death. Alas, the claws of death had not yet finished with us, reaching out to take our beloved Nana a year after Michael's death and her husband, our grandfather, eighteen months later. A new ritual had arrived after Michael's death. Mum would take all of us to Glasnevin cemetery every Sunday afternoon to visit the grave of Michael, and later our Gran and Grandad. For us, this would go on for years and we never showed any reluctance or voiced any complaints, again, for fear of upsetting mam. I so disliked those afternoons and always endeavoured to avoid looking at and reading the inscriptions, as we passed the countless graves. If I spotted the grave of a baby or teenager, it upset me for the day. As we got older, we found there were other things we wanted to do on bright sunny Sunday afternoons. We would not, for fear of hurting our Mum's feelings, mention this to her, but in time, we dropped off visiting, one by one. Our eldest brother had now left home. Mum went alone, but some Sundays her sister would accompany her there. Soon after our brother's death, yet another obstacle had arisen.

Like a mountaineer trying to reach the peak of Everest, thus started our mother's journey to reach 'The Holy Grail', but in Mum's case, not an endeavour to reach the top of a mountain and place a flag, no, but, in effect, it turned out to be almost as difficult. Her aim was to buy and place a tombstone above the grave of her golden boy and her parents. She scrimped and saved every penny in her endeavour to reach her goal. Ah, but the boulders of preventability blocked every inch of her path along the way, a case of two steps forward and four back! Mum was not reaching for the stars in the form of a large fancy headstone, even she knew that was an aim that would never be achieved, no, just a plain simple stone bearing the names of her parents and son. With now six children at home, it naturally meant every year there was a child to be dressed for Confirmation and Communion, as well as items like shoes and other necessities. And, still, the Sunday ritual continued, the visits to the grave in Glasnevin cemetery. From her weekly visits, our mother became so acquainted with the owners of graves in and around Michael's grave, she was now on first name terms with them. The grave of Greta's husband was directly behind ours. Even after all these years I remember the large black marble heart with the name 'Joe' emblazoned in white on it's centre, and a broken zig zag line to indicate a broken heart. Years later, I recalled one Sunday afternoon when Mam returned from her visit to the grave. Rushing in, we could see she was very upset. 'What's the matter?' we asked 'Oh, I can't believe it. When I arrived, I could see Joe's grave was dug over and I went to read the glass shades and found Greta's name on them.' 'Who's Greta?' we asked. 'Why, you must remember Greta, Mrs Byrne, her husband Joe is buried directly behind our Michael. I wish I had known, I would have attended.'

Mam left the room to find her every day overall, but came rushing back, blessing herself. 'Sweet Jesus. I have just had a dreadful thought! Both Greta's children live abroad, young Joe in New Zealand and Maura in America. Who's going to visit the grave now?' How could one not love and adore such a woman? Mr Mickey Clifford was a grand man, an unassuming man, unaware of the esteem and respect the people of the street held him in. A quiet chap who was always ready to help, he would fix bicycles, mend toys, help the lads to make buggies, and do all sorts to help anyone. I think he was a carpenter by trade. It was he who came up with the idea of making a surround for the grave. It consisted of several lovely carved wooden posts, linked together with a white chain. He would also make a wooden crucifix that would bear the family names on a central brass plaque. Bless him, a couple of months later Mum made her usual journey to the cemetery to find the job not only completed, but also erected and in place. Nothing amateurish or home made looking about this chap's work. It was indeed beautiful, if one could use that term about a grave's surround. And there, sparkling at the centre of the cross, was a brass plaque, bearing the names of our brother and grandparents. She had reached her Everest and, finally, 'The Holy Grail' she had set her heart on, despite the many obstacles along the way. But, as seen, she would never have achieved her heart's desire without having met a good Samaritan, Mr Clifford, along the way. It would last for many years but, in time, the Irish weather would eventually cause the wood to perish and deteriorate. And we were back to square one. However, we the family were in a somewhat better position than we had been all those years before. We, the older ones now, were working and contributing to the household. Mum started yet another effort to get a headstone, and eventually was able to afford a very small stone, with the names of her loved ones engraved on it. It is no bigger in size than a computer. It is dwarfed all around by beautiful headstones. The grave itself is hard to find in

109

the vastness that is now Glasnevin, and that particular plot almost covered with high grass. A person could almost trip over it, unless they were aware it was there. But we know exactly where it is. When our father returned home, he, like thousands of others, could not find work, just an odd day of casual labour on the quays.

He went to England and worked there for many years, coming home to his family when he could. He begged our Mam to leave Dublin and join him but, she always made an excuse not to do so. I suspected she could not bear thinking there would be no one to visit the grave of her beloved son and her parents every week, as she had done for years. Eventually, Mam did come to England to join her family, but she still returned at regular intervals to visit the grave, accompanied by a younger sister who had remained in Dublin. I could not even begin to imagine the pain she must have felt, as she stood there over the grave of her loved ones. I could not help thinking, Mam, your body may be buried in England, but your heart lies here.

Chapter Eighteen
Bountiful

While memories are not preserved like old photographs, I am finding, as I travel back down memory lane, dents in my recall, that I can reluctantly only put down to old age. However, is that not to be expected considering the events and happenings I write about what happened, oh so long ago. I had already written the following story many years ago but, on rereading it, realised I had the whole concept of its subject, Bridget, my mum's sister, oh so wrong. If all the facts of Bridget's life story were put into print, it would fill a book. I can only relate what I learned from my own Mam and some tit bits from my Grandparents, Bridget's parents. Reasons for some of the happenings are lost to me and I can only hazard a guess at events that took place, but the following I know to be true. In the Dublin of the 1900s, my Grandparents were living in very poor circumstances. Their abode was in the north side Dublin tenements. They had four children, Mary, known as Mamie, Julia, my Mam, known as Lou, Bridget, known as Bridie, and, lastly, Patrick, naturally, known as Paddy! My Grandfather earned a living as a shoe/boot maker, at a time when shoemakers were ten a penny. Now, my Grandfather had a sister named Kate who had left Ireland many years before and, over the years, had risen to become matron at a large hospital in the north of England. She, Kate, had never married and had done extremely well for herself. On one of her rare visits home, she called to see her brother, my Grandfather, who she was very fond of. I guess she must have been appalled at what she encountered. The crumbling tenements, the lack of sanitary conditions and the picture as a whole. Whatever the reason, she offered to take Bridget back to England with her. According to the 1911 census, Bridget was four years old, but I do not know what age she was when her parents agreed to let her go to live with her Auntie Kate in England. I suspect she was very young. Time and time again, I have asked myself how Bridget's parents could agree to this. Did they make the sacrifice of letting her go knowing she would be assured of a better life in England? On the other hand, I ask myself, why would a settled maiden woman take on the responsibility of a young child when she herself had a very busy and responsible position, but no experience of children, apart from the children she would come into contact with at the hospital. I shall never know the answer. Chalk and cheese, night and day comes to mind here! Bridget's life changed dramatically from the life she had shared with her siblings back in Dublin. Kate, her new guardian, was of another world. Reserved, church going, a member of the Catholic ladies sewing circle, amongst other things. I don't think Bridget would have had children her own age to play with, apart from those she encountered at school. Bridget was brought up by the rules Kate adhered to, rules she considered correct but to my mind from a previous generation! Children will not speak unless spoken too, children will not eavesdrop on adult conversation, you will learn to manage the weekly allowance allotted to you, always act and dress in a reserved manner and, most importantly, correspond with your parents on a weekly basis, which Bridget did. Always a post card every week in a childish scrawl which gradually, and in time, became a beautiful script, one Bridget retained until her death. On reflection, I ponder and wonder, did her life change for the better? While materially yes, fine clothes, a fine and established household, a good education, but at what cost? Separation from her parents and siblings, not for her the joy of piccy beds, relieveo, playing shop, gathering and eating winkles, oh, so many childish games known and loved by Dublin children. I do not know why, when or what year

112

Bridget returned home, a young woman. Had Kate become too old to manage and have the responsibility of Bridget? Did she, Kate, feel she had given her every advantage possible and it was time for her to be reunited with her parents? Did Kate think the cygnet had become a fully-fledged swan, and was now ready to fly out into the world under her own steam? Ah, so many ifs and buts, with questions that will never be answered. The following is our mother's account of her arrival back to Ireland: 'Oh, we were all so excited! Our Mother and Father could hardly contain themselves. We, the family all dressed up in our best Sunday clothes and took the train to Kingstown to meet the boat. We watched as the passengers disembarked, but there was no sign of our Bridget. My Mother fretted in case she had missed the boat. But then we saw her, the last passenger to disembark. A vision in a white lace dress, caught at the waist by a large white satin sash. On her feet dainty satin shoes and white hose. She also carried a white lace parasol that matched her dress. She was confidently issuing orders to a porter who dragged her heavy trunk behind her. We kissed and hugged on the quay side and, after the porter had left, she ordered her younger brother Paddy to 'see to my trunk.' Perhaps it was the imperious manner of her request, but Paddy refused to obey her order. Bridget carefully proceeded to let down her beautiful parasol, folding it carefully into its pleats and tied it up. She then proceeded to whack her younger brother on the backside calling him a 'common street urchin.' I don't doubt the faces of my Grandparents would have turned to one of dismay when they realized the size of the trunk ruled out a return trip home on the train! An expensive cab was required to accommodate the large trunk. What, I wondered, were Bridget's thoughts as the journey took them home, passing through the salubrious areas of Kingstown and Dun-Laoghaire, the large houses and beautiful gardens. Did she think she was coming home to similar surroundings, or had her guardian, Kate, given her some inclination of what to expect? How could one calibrate the effect and shock she felt on arrival at the slums that was to be her home? She dressed and spoke differently and had interests not shared by her siblings, truly a fish out of water! By now her two sisters were working in Jacob's biscuit factory while Bridget elected to stay home reading her favourite books and eating copious amounts of her favourite grapes. She was so set in her ways, and while she loved her parents and siblings, she had no wish to socialise with others. Her faith was strong and would remain so for the rest of her life. On one occasion, her father got an order to make a fine pair of boots, but did not have the money to purchase the makings of them. He hummed and hawed before reluctantly asking Bridget for a short loan to buy the materials required. Bridget did loan her father the money, but only after informing him, 'Father, you really must learn to manage your financial affairs and situation better than this. You must learn to set aside a certain sum for such occasions.' This, directed at a family that were living hand to mouth! Kate had indeed taught her well. Ah, but Bridget had a lot to learn! Welcome home to a world of sharing a house with other families, sharing one toilet with many others, washing under a cold tap in the outside yard, amongst other things. In time, she would reluctantly join her two sisters working at Jacobs, but while her two sisters joined in the then popular tea dances and outings run by the factory, she, Bridget, abstained from doing so. She preferred to stay home with her parents and her beloved books. In time, both her sisters and one brother would marry and have families. Bridget did eventually meet John, her future husband, but according to my Mam, not before she returned the engagement ring four times! She was aged twenty six when she married. I do not know how or where they met. As children, and later grownups, we, her sister's children, adored Uncle John. A man of rare integrity and simple honesty, he absolutely adored Bridie, as she was now called.

The name Bridget was lost somewhere along the way! John had held the same job since he was a youth. Marriage did not interfere with the easy going way Bridie had adopted. The pattern of her life would remain the same. Her time was her own and she spent it doing what she wanted and loved to do. She led a simple life; her parents and siblings were her life. Her day always started by Mass attendance, then everyday visits to her parents and her sister Lou, our mother, who lived in the same house. She and John always lived close by and within walking distance to her old home. Bridie and John never had children of their own, but were indeed oh so generous to all of us, their nieces and nephews, buying us socks and shoes, a great help to our parents. Bridie never changed her mode of dress for as long as I can remember. She never needed a perm, having nice curly hair. She was about five foot two and plumpish, but not overweight. She always wore a gaberdine coat, flat sensible shoes and always a beret on her head, conservative in her dress and manner. Oh! And how could I forget her shopping bag! A strong square of rexine with handles. I had never ever seen her without it, glued to her arms never to be divorced from! Yet, it became apparent that while she abhorred anyone knowing her business, or that of the family, she herself loved to stop and talk to others and learn of all their business. It would normally take about fifteen minutes to walk from her home to that of ours, but because of her love of gossip and talking to everyone along the way, it could take an hour or more! I had never heard her use a swear word and the only indication she was angry or annoyed would be when, through her dress, she placed her two thumbs under the top of her laced up corset and pulled it even further up! Along the years, she had lost the refined English accent, although not completely. She was perhaps not as broad as her sisters and brother. I guess, although her life had changed completely, some of the earlier expectancies and indulgences she had experienced while living with Kate still clung on and appeared through the

present day mists, like a lightning rod from the past. I think
she thought house work was beneath her and carried it out
reluctantly. She would bring her washing down to Mam
saying, 'My small wash is not going to make much
difference to your load.' I should mention Mam's load
consisted of washing for eight children, herself and Da, plus
her aged mother and father! And, despite all of this, the love
shared by these two sisters was something to behold, even
though their characters could not be more different. She
would accuse Mam of being 'too flaithiulach' (generous).
'You will never have anything.' While she herself would
never pass a beggar in the street without giving them
something. When she arrived at our house the famous
shopping bag would be opened and out would come all sorts
of goodies, always something for her mother and father: ten
cigs for my Da and a sponge cake and large block of cheese
for Mam and us children. On arrival at our house, she
would remove her hat and coat and settle down comfortably
in the one and only easy chair. She would expect Mam to
drop everything and sit and talk to her, a luxury Mam could
not afford in her everyday busy life. She loved it if none of
us children were present, constantly reminding Mam, 'Little
children have big ears.' If we arrived home from school for
lunch, she would tell us to go out and play, despite the fact
it would be lashing down outside! Mam would take her to
task, telling her, 'Leave the children alone, they are only
home for lunch and they are certainly not going out to play
in the rain.' 'Ah, then, I shall ramble over to Halson Street
church and say a few prayers until they (us) have gone back
to school.' She would expect her sister to drop everything
and sit and gossip. Of course, it did not happen, not with the
washing and ironing that mounted from four adults and
eight children. And, because we children were present,
normal conversation would cease and the phenomenon of
Bridget's language would take its place! 'Lou, you will never
guess who I met on the way down here.' 'Who?' 'M. T.'
'Who's M.T?' 'You must know M.T. She's the one married

116

K.W.' 'Eh, no, I don't know who you're talking about.' 'Of course, you do, the mother in law's S. J. (making a slashing motion across her stomach) that had that big operation.' And, so it would go on, Bridget never ever mentioning a name because some of us little pigs with big ears were hanging about! She, Bridie, wanted Lou, our mother, all to herself. Mam, always up to her eyes in washing or cleaning, had no time for this nonsense and most of the time did not even know who Bridie was referring to, much to the latter's annoyance! 'It's getting late, isn't it time you went home to prepare John's dinner?' 'Ah, no, he'll be grand, I left everything prepared.' Mam would often remark Bridie must have gotten the lovely John out of a lucky bag! I can't even imagine Bridie's reaction when John came home with the news that the firm he had worked for all those years had closed down. He, and all the other workers, were now redundant. They had never envisaged such a happening, feeling safe and secure by the fact his seniority and the number of years working there, had felt like a band of permanence that could never be broken or ended. Despite going out every day looking for work, there was none to be had. A reluctant John joined the army, as did our own father who was in the same position. It would be three years before John saw his beloved Bridie again. I still have one or two post cards he sent her from far away places. It was during this period we lost our sixteen year old brother Michael. Da, now in Italy, could not get compassionate leave to return home. Mum had great support from all of her family and the laid back Bridie really came to the fore, showing a strength no one suspected she possessed. She, Bridie, had always favoured the delicate Michael. She was a tower of support and understanding and this despite the fact she did not have a maternal bone in her body. She would not even know how to feed or hold a baby, especially a crying one. Every Sunday, she, Bridie, would accompany our mother to the cemetery for years afterwards, even taking turns to buy the flowers. Bridie cut a lonely figure

117

and truly missed John. It was a long separation. She spent most of the day in our house with her mother, father and us, returning to her lonely room every evening. She still stopped to talk to everyone she knew on the way down to our house. I truly suspect some of the ladies who spied her coming along in the distance would duck into shops or hallways to avoid her! She would detain them for ages, but while her time was her own, they had families to attend to. Mam decided one of us girls should go home with Bridie every night to keep her company. We girls were supposed to take turns, but this did not always go to plan! We did not want to go home with our auntie, preferring to stay in the street playing with our friends. How selfish we were, but in mitigation, at our age we did not understand the meaning of lonesomeness or the heartbreak of missing a loved one. 'It's your turn to go.' 'Oh no it's not, I went last night.' Mam: 'I don't care who's turn it is, one of you will go and keep your voices down. Your auntie is just above in your Nana's room and she'll hear you and be upset.' The journey to her home in Hardwick Street would take in Dominick Street Church to 'say a few prayers for John and Da to come home safely' and through the lane at the side of the church for a quick visit to Matt Talbot's shrine on Granby Lane. On to the shrine of Saint Anthony, then situated at the back of Temple Street Children's Hospital, and finally to her room, almost opposite in Hardwick Street. On entering this small room at the top of the house, the first thing one noticed was the alter with its red votive light. It was covered by numerous statues, some I did not know, or had not even heard of! I clearly remember one of the statues depicted a man with a beard, dressed in long robes. In one hand he held a staff, while the other hand showed him lifting his robe that showed a badly cut or wounded knee, with copious amounts of blood pouring from it. A large dog stood by his side, licking the wound. 'Who's he,' I asked. 'What! Do you mean to tell me you don't know who this is? What do they teach you in that school? That is Saint Roc.' From that day

118

forward we children renamed this, to us, unknown Saint, Dickie Rock! My knees could not take any more kneeling, bless her. She looked so forlorn and lonely, as she knelt to utter a last few prayers. I feigned sleep! She was glad of our company every evening and, if she suspected a reluctance on our part, she would say, 'I'll tell you what.

I have some real butter at home and a nice crusty turnover. So, we shall call at the chip shop, (never chippy), and get a nice one and one between us, wouldn't you like that?' The level and intensity of her love for our mother was akin to the Japanese knot-weed, something that could never be removed. But she wanted the impossible, our Mam's undivided attention. There was no doubt she had odd ways and, as children, we were blind to the goodness emanating from this small, nondescript, little woman who was a part of our everyday life. She would invite some of us children to visit her in her rooms down in Sean Mc Dermot Street (where she now lived), to partake of some fruit. We would eagerly visit, climbing about five flights of stairs to get to her place at the top of the house, our older brother never failing to remark, 'We will have a nose bleed by the time we get there.' On arrival, she would give us an unopened jar of fruit jam and a couple of spoons and tell us we would find lots of fruit in the contents! Her prayers were answered and her husband John and our Da returned safely from the war. But yet, despite John's return, life went on as usual for Bridie. Apart from Sunday, her daily visits to see her parents and our family continued. We had now acquired a television set from Peats on the never, never and John would sometimes accompany her to watch his beloved westerns. We were all enthralled by this wonderful new addition and our small room took on the look of a mini cinema! Small children sat on the floor, adults on the few chairs and bigger children scattered around in whatever space they could find. As we grew older, Aunt Bridie took on a more protective role, questioning us as to our every move. 'Where are you going? Who are you going with? I hope it's

119

not with that young one from such a street, she's not a nice girl. Why, I even heard her swearing when I passed her the other day!' And, if we thought that was bad, what was to follow became a bad dream. We, now teenagers, would invite our 'fellas' home to meet our parents, having known them for some time, and of course the ever present Auntie Bridie. 'Mam, Da, this is Anthony Cassidy, This is Mam's sister our Auntie Bridie.' Bridie would instantly become alert and sit upright in her chair. Addressing Anthony, Bridie's interrogation would commence. 'How are you son? Tell me, are you related to the Cassidy clothes shop people?' 'Eh, no ma'am, I'm not.' 'Oh, I see.' (Big disappointment) 'Well, are you related to the Cassidy people that has the ironmongers shop on the south side?' 'Eh, no, I wish I was.' 'Well, what does your father do?' 'He works in the Glass Bottling Company, as I do.' 'Is it a steady job?' 'Well, my Da has worked there all his life and I've been there since I left school.' 'Ah, that's grand, I'm told that company pays very well. Are you on a good wage?' Aunt Bridie would be on the point of asking exactly what their wage was, or how much they earned a week, much to our horror. We would be making pleading eyes towards Mam to put a stop to this, as not only did it cause us huge embarrassment, as it did our parents. Mam would bring the interrogation to a close by telling Auntie Bridie to leave the young man alone and let him drink his tea! If we were taking anyone home, we only did so when we knew for certain Bridie was not present. Can one wonder why we girls were never invited on a second date, nor saw hide nor hair of the fellas again? I sometimes wonder how we all managed to marry with Auntie Bridie around, but marry we did. Our older brother would say he was convinced our auntie was the chief interrogator for the Third Reich! He had cause to be upset with Bridie as she had driven many a pretty girl from our door, telling them, 'Go on home, my nephew is too young to be having girlfriends.' In older years, we would reflect on her conduct and intrusions and arrived at the conclusion she wanted what was best for us. Boyfriends who had steady jobs who could support us and, for the boys, girls who would be good housewives and mothers. Sadly, her approach in these matters was akin to a bull in a china shop! Had Kate not included tact in her many teachings to the then young Bridie? Everything she did was done spontaneously and without solicitation. Age would bring with it a greater understanding of her, and, to us, her odd ways. When delved into and examined minutely the end result was always the same, producing the same answers, goodness on her part.

Everything she said and did was carried out with us, her sister's children, in mind. She was childless, but looked upon us as her responsibility, while lacking the required experience, perhaps a leftover of her days with the strict Kate, her former guardian from another world and place, now dead and gone. The following is a true story and, perhaps, an insight into the person who was our Auntie Bridie. Our wonderful neighbour, Mrs D, who lived at the top of our four storied house, ran several clubs which entailed giving out dockets that could be spent at shops like Bolger's, Cassidy's and so forth. They, the recipients, would call every week with repayments. Rather than climb the many stairs to the top of the house, they would leave the money with our Mam on the ground floor. Mam would hand over the payments to Mrs D, as she passed our door on the way to the shops. Mam, as usual, was busy ironing when her sister arrived on her usual daily visit. Bridie made herself comfortable, as she watched Mam go through her mountain of ironing, advising her, 'Why don't you just fold them, sure you'll just have to do it all over again in a couple of days.' I doubt it was concern for Mam and the hard work involved, but rather a case of annoyance that she did not have her sisters undivided attention! A couple of hours passed and Mam asked, 'Hush, do you hear a baby crying?' 'No,' replied Bridie, 'I don't.' A few minutes passed and again Mam said, 'I'm sure I hear a baby crying.' Bridie, now getting rather flushed, again said she did not hear a baby crying. Mam arrived at the conclusion some woman had gone to the top of the house to pay her club money and left the baby in the hall. 'I shall go out and shout up to let them know their baby is crying.' 'No, don't do that,' cried Bridie, but, too late, Mam had entered the hall to find a pram, old enough to have come from Noah's ark, with a crying baby inside. 'Don't shout up cried Bridie, he's mine.' 'Yours? What would you be doing with a baby? Sure, ya can't mind yourself, never mind a baby.' And the story unfolded according to Bridie. 'Well, after I left Mass this morning, I met Mrs Stephens. She's a great woman you know, and well in with the nuns. She does great work finding homes for the babies of the poor, unfortunate girls who land up in the homes. During the conversation, I happened to mention we, John and I, were childless and she asked me would I not consider taking a baby. She said it would be a grand Christian thing to do and, before I knew it, she took me off to the convent and it was all arranged in no time. Mind you, the nuns were very good and supplied the pram!' 'Oh my God! Have ya taken leave of your senses?' 'When did the baby have its last feed and change of nappy?' 'How would I know? What do I know about babies?' 'That's right, precisely nothing! You had no business taking it or letting Mrs Stephens talk ya into it. You must take the baby back.' 'Ah, Lou, your right, but I would feel very bad about taking it back, would you not keep him?' At this my Mam exploded! 'Do you not think I have enough to do with eight of my own and me mother and father to take care of? Me mother is gone into her second childhood and I can't take me eyes off of her for fear of her rambling off. No, you took the poor infant and you will go and make arrangements for its return, the cheek of ya!' It would take about a week for the baby to be returned. We called him Martin and were delighted to have another baby in the house. We would not have to borrow a baby for our trips to the Phoenix Park, we had our very own! But, despite the pleadings of us girls, the

122

baby was returned. That event occurred in, I think, the early forties. A time when it was normal to take on someone's child, without investigation into circumstances or background by the authorities. One has only to read up on Dublin's social history to find this was not a rare occurrence. Abandoned babies, taken in and raised by poor families who could ill afford to do so, bless them. Several years had passed. Da is still working in England. Four daughters and two sons are now married, also living in the U.K. and raising their families. Michael, our youngest brother, will not leave Dublin and is now married with his own family. May is homesick and decides to go back home. Mam is still living in our old tenement house with our youngest sister.

For years, Da had begged our mother to come and live in England, pointing out almost all the family are now there. But our grandparents were still alive in the earlier years and no way would our mother leave them in their declining years, they so depended on her. When her beloved mother died and her father the following year, there was now no excuse for Mam not joining her family. Ah! But what about Aunt Bridie? How could she leave her beloved sister who was now a widow? They were a whole together, one inseparable unit, joined not only by flesh and blood, but also by a deep love for each other. How in God's name could they be separated into two halves? The answer came in the form of a letter informing Mam and the two other families in our house they were to be rehoused. According to our Mam, no way were they going to move her out 'to the country'. She was an inner city girl, born and bred. And, according to Bridie: 'Ah Lou, there's your answer, we would be separated anyway, with me having to get two or maybe even three buses, depending where they send you.' Go to England. Although heartbroken, Bridie encouraged Mam to join her family, telling her, 'Am I not old and ugly enough to look after myself? You have a husband and family over there and, after all these years, you owe it to them to be with them and, don't forget, isn't our brother Paddy also over there. Ah, you'll be grand.' May, our sister who had returned to live in Dublin, assured our Mam she would look after Bridie and despite having a young family of six girls, she was an absolute star. We, the family, cannot praise May highly enough for the care she gave to her auntie Bridie. She, May, stepped in where Mam had left off. May's home was now the one Bridie went to every day. May was the one who visited Bridie in hospital every day on the occasions when she was admitted. And, naturally, May was the one who did her washing as she passed it over with the words, 'My small load won't make much difference to the pile you have.' Now, where had we heard that before? Bridie was not easy to look after, her odd ways became even more apparent, yet May soldiered on, doing everything she could for her. She would gradually decline, no doubt missing her beloved Lou. The removal men arrived ready to take Mam's and some of her mother's stuff for transport to England. Our nannies three foot shades, that housed statues of the blessed Virgin and the Sacred Heart, caused Mam untold worry. She danced up and down the path crying, "Be careful, for God's sake, watch how ya carry them, there me mother's shades and statues.' And this, despite having about four blankets wrapped around nannie's shades to protect them on the journey! They arrived at their new home intact. Mam moved to a house two doors up from me. Just Mam, Da and our youngest sister. Our sister would marry, thus leaving them on their own and, I like to think, they were happy with their family living all around them. I know our father was, he loved to have their many grandchildren calling. I did not have what one would call a pal. Mam was my pal and we went and shared everything together. We shopped together, went to the washhouse together and both looked forward to our once-a- week bingo. One week she got a full house and rather than shout, 'House', whispered across the table to me, 'That's me.' But, by then, the caller had called the next number and she lost

124

the claim. 'Mum,' I chided her, 'Why didn't you shout really loud?' 'What! And have all these people looking at me? Will ya go on outa that.' She would return to Dublin several times to visit her sister Bridie whom she constantly worried about. And, on her return, I would always detect a sadness about her. I would ask myself was the sadness because she was leaving her sister yet again, or because she missed her own people and surroundings. When we, her children, had left Dublin we had been young adults, ready to take on the world and any adventure we might encounter: new people, new places, nothing phased us. I asked myself had she remained would she not have faced the same problems? A new house in a place she was unfamiliar with, the loss of all her old neighbours and friends. Her youngest daughter would have married and she would then be left on her own. While here, in a different country, she had a nice comfortable two bedroomed house with every facility that the tenements had never afforded her.

And, we, their children all around them. Was she missing the Sunday visits to Glasnevin Cemetery with Bridie, something they had done every Sunday for donkey's years? Did she feel she had deserted her beloved late son Michael? She was never lonely, we made sure of that. It soon became clear when she announced, 'I'm going back home and I shall take Bridie back here with me.' We pointed out that she was not getting any younger, nor was my Da, and were worried could she, even with our help, cope? Bridie arrived back with Mam to her home in the north of England. She loved the house and especially the garden. Da made her welcome and she settled in. Mam gave her small tasks to do which not only made her feel useful, but also very important. It would sometimes take hours for her to do a simple task, but she was left to it and could sometimes be heard humming along to a song on the radio, as she got on with her 'job'. Three old people sat warm and comfortable, as they sat many an evening reminiscing of the old days, of people they had known, but now long gone. There would be lots of, 'Do you remember,' and, 'Whatever happened to...'. Paddy, their brother, who was then still living just twenty minutes away, would call every Sunday afternoon to visit his sisters. How they loved and doted on their younger brother, fussing and flapping over him like mother hens! Our Da collapsed and died of a heart attack, he had worked hard all of his life and now, when they should have been relaxed and enjoying life, he was gone. In time, Bridie's health would decline and our aged Mam was unable to look after her and she was placed in a home, within walking distance. She had no problem adapting to her new surroundings. In fact, she loved to sit in the lounge with all of the other ladies gossiping and finding out their business, while never disclosing to them any of her business. Old habits die hard! We would visit her all the time, remembering her goodness to us as children. When we visited, we would bring her favourite fruit and sweets, BUT, if we dared to offer any of the nearby ladies a sweet, she would go mad telling us, 'They don't share theirs.' Mam had a love of flowers and as a treat I took her to the famous Southport Flower Show. It had started out a fine day, but around noon the heavens opened. We dashed for shelter under one of the big tents, where we endeavoured to eat our packed lunch. I can't remember why we started laughing, perhaps because we looked like a couple of drowned rats, but my did we laugh, we just could not stop. I can't remember having laughed so much. The rain ceased and we had the most wonderful day, walking around admiring the beautiful displays. A beautiful, unforgettable day and one that will remain in my mind forever. On the way home on the bus, Mam complained about a pain in her back. I suggested she sleep at my house that night and, when we arrived home, I put her to bed with a hot water bottle. I left a little bell by her bedside and told her to ring it during the night if she was in pain or needed me. It rang at about eight o'clock the following morning and when I entered her bedroom, she was in great pain. 'Mam, why didn't you ring the bell during the night.' 'I did not want to disturb anyone.'

126

I called a doctor who called an ambulance and my darling beloved Mam was rushed into hospital. I sat with her holding her hand in the A&E department. A priest entered and proceeded to give Mam the last rites. 'Am I dying? asked Mam? 'No, Mam,' I lied. 'They have done away with that and replaced it with a blessing for the sick, everyone is given it if they are poorly.' I could not bear to see my Mam frightened. They moved her to a side ward but I was not allowed to go in with her. How I wanted to be with her to hold her hand and tell her how loved she was. After what seemed to be hours, the doctors came to tell me they could not save her, she had died of a massive heart attack. That was the moment my world fell apart, not just mine, but also that of the family who I had phoned and were with me in the waiting room. How touched we, the family, were when two wreaths arrived for the funeral, one from the offices where she had cleaned in Dublin and the other from the dealers in Moore Street, many of them old neighbours. Of course, we did not tell Bridie of her beloved sisters death. What was the point of upsetting her.

When we visited her and she asked, 'Where's your Mam,' we would make all sorts of excuses as to Mam's absence. She, Bridie, never questioned us and just accepted what we told her. Shortly after attending the funeral, their only brother retired and went back to his family in Dublin. Bridie contracted pneumonia and died in hospital and strangely their brother Paddy died the same year. Almost to the day, the two sisters and only brother died the same year. We buried Bridie with Mam and Da. And under her name we put the inscription, 'Not just our aunt, but a very special person'. We know, this is what she would have wanted, to be together with her beloved sister, Lou.

Chapter Nineteen
An Unravelled Yarn

'Marie Leonard, come to the top of the class and show the pupils your work.' Marie left her desk, a satisfied smirk on her face, as she sallied forth clutching the needles and maroon coloured piece of knitting she was working on. Holding aloft the yard long sample, Sister Regis invited us, the class, to notice the perfect tension of the neat rows of plain and purl stitches and perfectly straight edges, with not a dropped stitch in sight! I swear she looked directly at me as she uttered the words, 'dropped stitches'! The sewing class had already graduated from learning how to do the tack and hem stitch and had now entered the puzzling world of knitting. The pupils were issued with small balls of various coloured wool and shown how to cast on stitches, continuing to the required length in rows of one line of plain and one line of purl, before finally casting off. The words domestic science had not yet entered our vocabulary. I cowered even further down in my desk, hopelessly endeavouring to hide what had commonly come to be known throughout the whole school as, 'the bottle shaped scarf'. I had gotten off to a fairly good start, to my mind, even though it took all of my strength to get a needle between the stitches, I had cast them on so tightly! Sadly, after about five inches of knitting was completed (holes included), I had somehow gone astray and dropped several stitches from both sides, thereby leaving me with a piece of work that resulted in a perfect bottle shape. Hence the name! I unravelled and re-knit that piece of work so often it looked as though every rat in our street had chewed on it. Sister Regis was not amused, as at the end of the class year

all these pieces had to be unravelled, ready for the following year's pupils. Oh my shame and embarrassment, as it was pointed out to me what expert knitters and sewers my two sisters were, 'a credit to your mammy'. I pondered over this, as while me Ma could cook and clean with the best of them, she could not knit if it were to save her life! Crochet, yes, but Ma did not even know how to hold a pair of knitting needles! I heaved a sigh of relief as we left that class, glad to see the back of my bottle shaped scarf. Although I liked Sister Regis, despite everything, she was great. Ah, had I but known what lay ahead of me. Our next class up, and I inwardly shuddered as the voice of Sister Anthony, our new sewing teacher informed the class: 'Now children, as you have learned how to knit in your last class and are familiar with the different stitches and terms, we are going to learn how to knit socks. This will be done on four needles and you will be required to bring the following materials.' I visibly paled, recalling my difficultly with the simple scarf, when I couldn't manage two needles never mind four! Oh God, why couldn't they lower the school leaving age to eleven instead of fourteen, then I wouldn't have to go through this torture? I timed my request for knitting needles and several ounces of wool badly! One sister had just beaten me to it with a request for ingredients for the cookery class, while yet another required half a yard of linen for the sewing class she had just entered. Mammy, I have to have four knitting needles and some dark wool. Sister Anthony said so.' 'You want needles and wool, the other one wants flour, butter and sultanas, and another, material! Just who do those nuns think I am, Rothschild?' (I didn't dare ask who or what Rothschild was). 'But mammy 'You can 'but mammy' all you want. I haven't got the money and that's the end of it and tell the nun I said so.' 'But I can't go into school and say that to the nun.' (Very crossly) 'Well now, would you like me to go over to the school and I'll tell her?
I'll soon tell them I don't know where the next meal is coming from, never mind needles and wool!' I started to cry

and Ma's sister the ever present, eccentric Auntie Bridget tried to console me. 'Hush now, your mammy hasn't got the money to buy these things. Sure, we'll try and get you them from somewhere.' Some days later, she arrived at our house with the ever-present Rexene shopping bag and a smile on her face. 'Well now, sure didn't I tell you Saint Anthony was good? He'd never let you down. You have nothing to worry about, I got you the wool.' This broken heart was instantly mended; I could not wait to see what colour wool she had bought and wondered, had she got me the needles as well? Oh God, was she never going to take off her hat and coat, and couldn't she wait to gossip with Ma until after she had shown me the precious wool? I waited patiently; she could be so awkward and get on her high horse if I started to hurry her. 'Do you have little nail scissors?' she asked my mammy, as she reached into her shopping bag, withdrawing the largest khaki coloured jumper I had ever seen! 'Now, she said, as she looked towards my astonished face, we'll start on the sleeves first, you unravel one while I do the other. I'll start it off for you.' This then was my introduction to something that would haunt me for the rest of my school life! We unpicked, it broke, we knotted, we unpicked, again the wool broke and we knotted it yet again, and so it went on and on until finally, late into the night, we finished and were left with a ball of wool as big as a football!! I should mention here that by now, because of the huge number of knots sticking out all over the giant ball, it now looked like a giant hedgehog. You will also have gathered that Auntie Bridget, like mammy, was not a knitter! Why we never made it into small manageable balls I will never know, but reasoned at least it would be an acceptable colour for socks; didn't soldiers wear khaki socks? I had read somewhere that little girls in England were knitting socks and balaclavas for soldiers in the war. My imagination kicked in and a picture of a little girl, working her fingers to the bone, knitting socks to keep the troops warm, emerged. Eyeing the huge ball of wool, I reckoned not only would I knit a pair of socks for my daddy, but also a pair for Uncle John, with enough wool left over to make socks for a whole garrison! I could almost visualise the headlines in the Herald and Mail! Little Irish girl breaks all records by knitting 200 pairs of socks for the troops!! Ah, but in my eagerness, hadn't I forgotten something? Er, if I hadn't managed to complete one horrible little scarf, how ever was I going to manage all those socks? I can and I will sprang to mind. Sure, weren't my sisters grand knitters, they would help me. I was yet to find out that we were not allowed to take our work home from school. On that first day in our new sewing class, I watched as my fellow pupils removed the virgin balls of wool from their bags; small balls of black, navy and assorted shades of brown, the paper seals, still unbroken, holding the wool in place. It took both of my hands to remove the huge ball of khaki wool from the bag Auntie Bridget had supplied me with. The eyes of Ann O'Malley, the girl who shared my desk, almost doubled in size when she caught sight of it. Her whispered 'Jesus, Mary and Joseph' turned into a loud snigger, causing the rest of the class to turn around. Gasps, followed by loud laughter, caused Sister Anthony to call for silence. She approached my desk to find out the cause of the disruption in her class and I could discern a lifting of her eyebrows on catching sight of my ball of wool. I had made up my mind to repeat (should she question me) what Ma had said about telling the nuns, 'I haven't got the money for wool and needles.' Of course, leaving out the bit about who did they think mammy was, as I couldn't remember the name she had mentioned. (Rothschild). I had learned to my cost not to repeat word for word of what Ma said, after going into school and telling Mother Imelda Ma's words, 'Sod off and tell them nuns I haven't enough to feed the white babies never mind the black ones.' Looking back now, I think Sister Anthony was a wise old woman who at a glance took in the monstrous wavy ball of wool and probably guessed the reason behind it! Saving me further

embarrassment, she loudly proclaimed for the benefit of the class, 'Sure that's a grand big ball of wool Bridget.
Now I'm sure you'll get several pairs of socks out of that.'
Sister Anthony patiently taught us how to cast stitches on to four needles and of course, as usual, I cast them on so tight I struggled from one needle to the next. Tongue out, eyes down, I would manage to knit the stitches from one needle with great difficulty, but always managed to drop stitches before reaching the next, thus, more unpicking! Months into our new class, my classmates were well ahead of me, having already knitted a length of tubular work and were now ready to 'turn the heel', while I was still on the rib! By the end of the term, while all of the class were by now drawing the wool through to finish the toe of the sock, I had just about managed to get past the rib and completed about two inches of plain and purl. It was time to move on to the next class up, and sadly my now hated appendage (that's what it felt like) came with me. I was not given or allowed a 'pass', never having completed one sock, never mind a pair. And still it stuck, accompanying me all the way until I had completed my education at the ripe old age of fourteen! My dreams of supplying socks to the whole Western Front (my own personnel war effort) lay in ruins. I had visions of hundreds of soldiers dying of frostbite and all because I had never managed to learn how to knit socks! On leaving day, we were told to clear our desks and take any unfinished sewing or knitting work home with us. I had hoped to forget my, by now, famous ball of wool, but was given a kindly reminder by the head boarder. 'Bridget.' (titters) 'Don't forget your lovely ball of wool!' At that time, hand ball was a very popular game in Dublin. I had to pass the Ball Alley by Green Street on my way home. The playing area was surrounded by high railings. I stopped by the railings and removed the still huge ball of wool from its bag. Standing on tiptoe, I tied one end of the wool to one of the bars and proceeded on home leaving a trail of wavy, knotted khaki wool in my wake. I went up Little Britain Street and almost

as far as Capel Street before I felt it snagging and, looking back, saw a group of small boys following its trail... 'Hey, young fellas, do ya want a football', I shouted, as I threw it up and kicked it in their direction, just as I had seen my brothers do. Two days later I started work and went out into the wide world happy to have left the nightmare khaki ball of wool behind!

Chapter Twenty
Josie

Memory is such a strange thing. It comes upon one unbidden, sometimes fragmented, and not unlike a shattered pane of glass. While some pieces are easily put back together, the smaller fragments can't be fitted, no matter how hard one tries. I ask myself are those tiny pieces really memories we have no wish to recall and ones we purposelessly disperse, or perhaps are drowned and washed away with a million tears? I am glad my next memory is whole, one that brings love to the heart and, yes, a smile to my face. Dublin 1940 It was only when I was old enough to play out on the street, that I first met Josie. We, as innocent children, never noticed anything different about this girl, well, apart from the fact that to us she was a big girl and we children always looked up to the (older) big girls. We loved her, as she was always ready to partake of our childish games and agreed to fit in with anything we wanted to do. Josie would be in her teens, a tall gangling figure with twisted teeth, glorious hair and a warm smile. We would be a lot older before we realised dear Josie had somehow dodged the bullet of normality and was trapped between two spheres, in a place that was neither childhood nor adulthood. As we children played out on a summer's evening, our mothers would sit outside the doors of their tenement houses, sharing titbits of gossip, usually about who had passed away, who had given birth, plus discussing other things not fit for young ears! If we ventured near the group, we would be told by one of the older women to, 'Lave yer mammy alone and go back and play with the other childer'. Josie would appear and join in our skipping game with cries of, 'Ah, will ya let's play, ah, go on will yez?' She would beg of us children, 'I'll even turn the rope.' She would enter into our games as an equal, the adult part of her suppressed, consigned to, and buried in the very basement of her being, forgotten even for a short time in the joy of the childhood games that played such a big part of our lives back in the 30s/40s. Suddenly, Josie would tire of the game, leave our group and ramble over to the group her mother was in, something we children were never allowed to do. Not being a party (as a child) to these groups, I of course never knew what Josie's input (if any) to the conversation was. On reflection, maybe she just wanted to be near and put her arm through that of her mother. An only child who lived with an aged mother, they shared a small room in one of the tenement houses that lined our street. While almost everyone had built a scaffold of sympathy around this child/woman, sometimes the odd teenage boy would make a derogatory remark and, depending on whether she was in her child or adult world, she would react accordingly. The former would bring forth expletives and a belligerence that would put a docker to shame, while the latter would bring on a quicksand of despair that would see her running home with streaming tears and cries of, 'I'm going to tell me ma on you.' How, as children could we comprehend or understand the world that Josie inhabited? This woman/child who would play marbles with us one day while the next day the deep humanity and feelings that were encased within this body would find her offering profound sympathy to a family suffering bereavement and even offering to go and collect the habit for the deceased person! Her familiar and well known mantra, 'I'm grand at going for the messages', helped out many an aged person of the street and was always rewarded with a couple of pennies, which were immediately spent in the corner shop on a toffee apple or a few honeybees.

Life with, and around, Josie became an ethical quagmire, like a pendulum swinging back and forth, back and forth, woman/child, child/woman. While she was indeed very good at, 'going for the messages', which made her feel very important and doing house work (in a fashion), other deficiencies were overcome with the help of her many relations who lived in the street. This help was sorely needed when her beloved mother passed away. The shock of losing her adored mammy sent her spiralling even deeper into her childish disposition, but with the help of relatives and neighbours the funeral took place and Josie returned to the small tenement room that had been her haven, her place of safety, yet, never more to feel the comforting arms, the ever open arms and soothing voice that whispered, 'Hush now, everything is going to be alright.' The years passed and while we children became young adults, leaving behind our piccie beds, skipping ropes and balls, the now adult in years Josie was left behind, still trapped in her own world, but with yet another generation of children to plead with. 'Ah, go on, I'll give ya one of me nancy balls if ya let me play chainies with ya.' In adulthood, my mind would often meander down memory lane, thinking of my childhood friends and neighbours who would have now long gone. I, of course, always wondered what had become of Josie. Was help sought for her as a child, when it was blatantly apparent, she had a problem? Bearing in mind the horrors of mental institutions and children's homes in those far off days, did her mother want to protect her only child from entry into one of these places, by not seeking help? Did she choose to ignore the accepted rule of civilized behaviour, in favour of her only child? A lone woman whose future would be saturated with constant worry and woe. No compromise corner to be found for her, with a wise old Solomon waiting to offer advice and answer questions. She, a loving mother, made her choice. She kept her beloved Josie. While life swells up like an ocean and carries us all on different paths and directions, it somehow leaves memory currents that manage to connect us to past events and people. One of my most memorable memories of Josie was as follows: Josie's greatest pleasure was to 'get the messages' for anyone who needed something from the shops. She had a great sense of direction and was familiar with all the shops and streets surrounding her own. The voice of Mrs Berry shouting from the end of the street, 'Josie, here young wan, I want ya to get me a few messages', would be completely ignored, even causing her to duck into one of the halls out of sight. According to Josie, 'That auld one never gives me a penny for getting her messages', an indication perhaps that she was in adult mode – to be able to work that out. Of course, she could not remember or retain a shopping list, so was always given a written list with the correct money wrapped inside and followed by strict instructions: 'Josie, don't let go of that and, only give it to the man or woman in the shop.' Her favourite customer was old Mrs Marney. While most people would give her a home-made shopping bag made of sacking, Mrs Marney, to Josie's delight, was the owner of a real straw shopping basket. She, Josie, would swagger off to the shops swinging this item from side to side for all the world to see! Josie strolled up the street one fine sunny day coming from the direction of Henry Street. Her arms were filled with small bottles of milk, leaving us kids wondering who in our street could afford such an amount. An excited Josie informed us that Woolworth's were giving away free bottles of milk. 'There's crates of them outside the shop, ya just go and take what ya want.' Well, never ones to miss a freebie, a gang of us broke all speed records arriving at Woolworth's in Henry Street quicker than you could say Jack Robinson! And, yes, there they were. Crate upon crate of small bottles, just like the ones we got at school. We helped ourselves, greed causing us to stuff them into pockets, under jumpers, as well as carrying all our arms could hold. Envisaging the delight on our mother's face at this unexpected windfall, we hurried home to dislodge our bounty, ready to make a return trip to avail ourselves of this most generous offer on the part of the store.

We had only got as far as Todd Burns on the corner of Jervis Street, when a booming voice shouted out, 'Ya little thieves, I've caught ya red handed.' And, there, blocking our path was the biggest policeman I had ever seen. Despite our pitiful cries and explanations of innocence, he gathered us all together to march us down to Store Street police station. The very mention of police station was enough to send us scattering in all directions, dropping our precious cargo in our haste to escape. Alas, my poor sister never managed to get away, as the giant in blue had her in a head lock! Breathless, on reaching home, I burst in crying, 'Mammy, come quick, the policeman has taken our Julia to the police station' 'Oh my God! What for?' 'Oh mammy, he said we stole milk from Woolworths' I said, while making the sign of the cross upon my throat, to assure my mother I was telling the truth, explaining how Josie told us the milk was free and, there for the taking. Grabbing her coat from behind the door my mother dashed down to Henry Street to rescue her beloved child from the hands of this monster! The pair had already reached Talbot Street, before Mum caught up with them. Already a crowd had surrounded them, remonstrating with the man in blue at his treatment of the small girl. 'I'm doing me duty and will broker no interference from the lot of ye.' Despite mum's explanation of what had happened he still insisted on taking the small Julia into Store Street police station accompanied by my now very angry mother. 'What's the charge?', asked the duty Sargent as he stood up and peered over his desk to get a look at the criminal. 'Sure, I caught the lot of them red handed, as they stole milk from outside Woolworth's store. Unfortunately, the other crowd managed to escape capture.' 'Are you trying to take the piss outa me? Now, feck off out there and catch some criminals and, don't be wasting me time bringing terrified little girls in here.' The above simple story is one I remember vividly. It was apparent some smart Alec had noticed Josie 'getting the messages' and, aware of her condition, had fed her the tale of the free milk. And the moral of this tale? If you ever come across another Josie in your travels, be warned and don't believe a thing she tells you, before checking it out. Like almost every street in Dublin, (apart from the more salubrious) one would see small groups of women standing outside hall doors, leaning on the railings, while having a gossip to break the monotony of days spent doing the same things over and over again. In a mixed group, the older ones usually wore the cross over apron, always in dark colours, with the inevitable white pipe cleaners attached to wispy strands of white hair, in an effort to encourage a kink or curl. Their younger counterparts wore smaller front pinnies, but not for them the old pipe cleaners. Oh no! The new silver coloured metal curler had arrived on the market and even our mammy put them in her hair, which I thought rather strange as to me she was very old, at least forty! As the Angelus rang out from Halson Street church they would disperse, rushing indoors to check on cabbage that already had the arse boiled out of it. The excitement was almost palpable! The street had become alive! What was happening? Women were standing in large groups while others ran around waving white sheets of paper! The reason soon became apparent. How could it not? While the majority had received letters, some had not. Dublin City Council wished to inform the recipients of the letters a decision had been reached to demolish the houses at some time in the future and the occupants of said houses would be rehoused in the new housing estates, springing up all around and outside the city centre. Names like Crumlin, Finglas and Ballyfermot were bandied about. She may have been old, but Kitty Kelly was seen racing up the street at a pace of knots, despite the fact she had informed the dispensary doctor she was unable to, 'even step outside me door, sir.' I think back then a person could get some small sum of money via the dispensary doctor. It would be a pittance. Kitty joined one of the groups. 'Holy Mother of God, what's going on? Me auld fella has gone out to see if he can get a bit of work and I can't wait for him to come home to know what's happening. Will one of yez read it for me?' Noreen McAnulla put her hand into her pinny pocket and withdrew her specks, the pair that were held together with sticking plaster across the bridge, causing her to appear as though she has one eye on her forehead while the other was in its normal place. Noreen pulled herself up to her full height and, in her best voice informed a now trembling Kitty of the plans for demolition. 'Well now Kitty, according to my chap', she never ever refereed to him as my fella, 'it would appear the places mentioned are a very long way out, several miles in fact.' Kitty, crossing herself asked, 'Does that mean if I go to one of them places, I'll have to get a bus back into town and will there be a Moore Street there?' 'Yes, of course, it will mean getting a bus back into town Kitty but...' (smiling superciliously and with a pitying look in Kitty's direction) I doubt very much if you will find a Moore Street there.' 'That's it then. The Corporation can shag off, if they think they are moving me out of me auld room that I've lived in this past forty years" Kitty walked away, wiping the tears away with the bottom of her cross over pinny. Looking back across those many years, I have come to the conclusion we were a simple, unsophisticated group of people who did not ask for much from life. A clean bed, a warm place, a full belly and, most importantly, a few shillings for the rent to keep a roof over our heads. Unexpectedly, we now found ourselves thrust into a dilemma, one that could be equated with the story of the donkey and the carrot! Replace the carrot with a brand-new home with extra bedrooms, ones very own private toilet and never having to share with several other families, as we now did. And, the icing on the cake! A bathroom with a real full-length bath! And, dare I mention, possibly even a garden. A dream we never thought we would achieve! And yet, unbelievably, hesitation on the part of many. How many sleepless nights came about, as people pondered and worried, as they wondered where their next steps and decisions would lead them? Could they afford the rent, how much bus fare would be required to get to work and schools? Would they be near to shops whose prices would compare to those of Moore Street? While some could save on bus fares by cycling into work, not many had the luxury of a cycle. Fear of the unknown was a major factor. What would new neighbours be like? And, the all-important question, would there be a pawn shop? So many ifs and buts. Sadly, a couple of the older women did not live to see the changes. They passed away keeping their memories of the street intact, consigned forever to a museum of dreams. As usual, I and a few of my now teenaged friends went to pay our respects to the lovely Mrs Marney, the little Scots lady whose dialect we found hard to understand, despite her having lived in this street, for as long as I could remember. This bird like figure who turned up hems on long dresses and skirts, would run up underskirts on her sewing machine, housed on the landing adjacent to her room. A queue had formed on the stairs, waiting to offer sympathy to the family and there in front of us, was Josie. I never really understood if she was aware of the sadness of the occasion, but she always said the required prayer over the deceased, blessed them with holy water and proffered her hand to family members while uttering the usual, 'Sorry for your troubles.' Was she copying what others did before her? I don't think so. The integrity, humanity, love and caring exploded from this bruised body naturally and, unsolicited, Josie, may have arrived on this earth with many needs, but had an abundance of the qualities that mattered. But who would not laugh when, directly behind her, we watched as she doused not only the deceased with the Holy Water but the whole bed! This would be the last time I would ever see this lovely innocent girl, Josie, but not the last I heard of her. I left home even before the demolition of the tenements commenced fully. Some families had already been rehoused in dribs and drabs. It was not the exodus I had visualized and, on my first return visit, while our house was still standing, others stood, partly demolished. I looked at the now half wall where we had endlessly bounced our balls with our dresses tucked into our knickers. The gaping windows looking out on to a street that now held secrets, never to be revealed.

Even with closed eyes, I could tell where houses had stood and the families who had lived there. I looked at the railings of the house where the C--- family had lived and remembered their small son climbing over those railings and falling to his death in the area below. I wanted to turn and run away. It felt as though I was opening a door to a hurricane of sorrow. Yet, I had loved this place where four generations of my family had lived. I was born and reared here. Back then, my world was an intoxicating mix of childish innocence, poverty and appalling cramped living conditions, as were those of all the families who had occupied this street in the heart of Dublin. And, yet, through it all the warmth, sharing and understanding that held us together, like an inviable rope, continues to shine like the brightest star in the sky. Dear God, I pray and hope that the families who have moved out will find happiness and contentment and, in time, make a better life for their families than the ones they had here. Unpleasant though they may be, I shall not allow my memories to be crushed underfoot and blown away like grains of sand. No, I shall hold them close to my heart and treasure them. My sister was visiting and, as always, we reminisced about our childhood street. I was eager to know whatever happened to Josie? 'Ah, when the street was demolished, Josie was given a single flat on the South side.' 'What! Why? She knew no one there. That's terrible, they would not understand her and her strange little ways.' 'Well, strangely enough she got lots of help and people accepted her into their midst. She certainty settled in and family kept an eye on her, but she had to learn her way around to go for the messages.' (laughs) 'Is she still alive? 'Will ya go on outta that! She's long gone, sure she was years older than us. Did I not tell you about her funeral? You have never seen anything like it. All the old neighbours from the street came from far and wide to attend and not only them, but loads of people from the South Side also attended. They brought her back to Saint Ann's, where she went for mass when she lived in the street. She honestly had a great turn out and it was grant meeting up with all the old neighbours. We had a great day.' Ah, Josie, reunited with your beloved mammy. Fly with the angels.

Chapter Twenty One
Moore Street

My memories of Moore Street go back a hundred years, lol. Well, it feels like that! While we kids loved the street, shopping there on a Saturday with our ma took on a new dimension. We older girls would argue as to whose turn it was to go. Stopping to talk to a lot of the dealers, most of whom lived in our own street, would have become a nice little outing, with an ice cream thrown in, until the word 'butcher' was mentioned! Whichever one of us was helping on the day, they would automatically think, 'Oh God, here we go again.' What character would Ma turn into today? My sister reported she thought she was accompanying Maureen Potter on last week's shopping trip and, in her words, 'I was just morto.' The street, as usual was a hive of activity with lots of auld ones carrying string shopping bags, busy poking into barrels of corned beef, soaking in brine. What a poster this would have made: WHAT NOT TO DO, by the health and safety brigade, who arrived years later. Ma joined them, poking away until she found the piece she wanted. Carrying the dripping joint, she entered the shop. 'Morning Jerry, how are ya and how is the Mrs?' 'Ah, there ya are. We're grand, both game ball, now what can I get ya?' 'Will ya weigh me that piece of meat and let me know the price?' Jerry places the meat on the scales while telling Ma, 'Ya have a good eye, that's a grand joint.' 'I'll let ya know how grand it is when ya tell me the price.' 'Right now, that will be 3/6.' 'What! Have ya gone fecking mad Jerry or what! Put yer glasses on, sure there's not enough in it to make a decent sandwich! Do ya think I'm one of them rich auld ones from Balls bridge, with money to throw away? Will ya go on outta that, I'll give ya half a crown for it" Jerry's face turned a paler shade of white than his shop coat and battle begins. 'Ah Mrs, I couldn't let it go at that, sure it would be more than me job is worth.' Ma pulls herself up to her full five feet two and somehow manages to adopt both a look of indignation and disdain, all at the same time, as I stand watching and thinking what a fine actress she would have made. Without doubt, she would have given Maureen Potter a run for her money! Addressing Jerry: 'Listen me auld son, do ya have any idea how long I've been coming into this shop and me mother before me? That was in yer father's time, God rest his soul. (Blesses herself) 'Holy Mother of God, if he knew the prices yer charging, he would be turning in his grave. Ah, the man hadn't a mean bone in his body!' Ma is now in dramatic mode and to further emphasise her point, she takes two steps back, sending the saw dust on the floor flying in all directions. Then, with a flourish that would give credit to Noel Purcell she announces, 'And, I'll tell ya another thing, yer da would always throw in a few ribs free of charge when ya bought a joint.' A now worn- out Jerry leans over the counter and indicates to Ma to come closer and, whispering in her ear, says, 'I'll let ya have it for 2/9, but keep it quiet Ma smiles, 'Ah, sure that's grand, I'll see ya next week Jerry.' I swear to this day I heard Jerry muttering under his breath, 'Oh God, I hope not.' We cross the road and meet Biddy Byrne coming out of the Maypole. Ma stops to talk and I hear snatches of the conversation. 'I'm telling ya Biddy, the shop is not the same since poor auld Mr. Brennan passed away.' Both women bless themselves.

'That young fella of his is losing the run of himself, he can be so awkward!' I take delight in knowing, it won't be my turn to go shopping with Ma the following Saturday.

Chapter Twenty Two
My Beloved Nana

As in the case of any small child, I was unaware of the difference between rich and poor, good quality clothes or cheap practical apparel, the difference in speech and so many other things unconnected to the magic of childhood. My world way back then was one of spinning tops, balls, dolls and playing with my friends in our street of tenement houses. The questions and 'wondering' would come when I grew older. Ma would only have to say, 'Go and ask your Nana, 'and I would take the stairs two at a time to reach the landing above our ground floor rooms, where my maternal grandparents lived. Stepping over the threshold of my grandparents' rooms was like stepping into another world. Within a heartbeat, I was transported back to a time of gentility, austere dressing and surroundings that I had only seen pictures of in books. It was hard to believe that this was the heart of the Dublin slums I grew up in. Years later, I would devour books to learn more of the history of our street. It came as no surprise to learn that because of its location in central Dublin, it had once, in another time, housed lords and ladies, barristers and indeed even a member of parliament. These wealthy owners had long since gone, and yet a small part of their expensive indulgence could still be seen here and there, amongst the now crumbling ruins. With age and hindsight, I look back and laugh at a small part of the legacy left behind by the houses past owners! The four storey dwellings were now home to as many as eight families, and each room was referred to as the front parlour, back parlour, drawing room, back drawing room, two pair front and top floor. Our family lived in the front and back parlour, while my grandparents occupied what was then called the front and back drawing rooms! I could not imagine anything more fitting for my Nana. It felt as though one of those grand ladies of long ago had just stepped out and my grandparents had moved into their rooms, sadly, not the case. They were very poor. The room was huge and high, still retaining the beautiful mouldings and cornices where the walls met the ceiling, although in parts crumbling, yet not detracting from its beauty. As one entered the room, the light from two long windows opposite the door, reaching from ceiling to floor, flooded the room with light. Long crisp cotton nets were held in place by pairs of brass 'tie backs', and to complete the look, in front of each window were two large brass flower pots, holding my Nana's beloved geraniums. The plants stood on tall narrow tables with spindly legs, just wide enough to carry them. The long sash windows no longer worked, but they could be raised and some strong object placed beneath to hold them open. One day, my Nana showed me how they were supposed to work. Opening two long wooden folding shutters just inside both windows, she pointed out the rusted weights and now perished ropes that worked the openings. I remember my excitement on being shown this 'secret place', and made up my mind there and then never to disclose this magic hiding place to my siblings! I loved everything about my granny's rooms, from the old sepia pictures on the walls to my favourite object, the fireplace. Even now, looking back, I shake my head and wonder at the cost! Only a very wealthy person could have afforded such opulence. A cast iron fireplace taking up the space of almost one wall, it now shone and reflected years of loving care with the black-leading brushes. What craftsmanship had gone into it's making! Scrolls, grapes and birds covered every inch of its surface, the grate itself set well back with several bars across its front.

A large brass fender, with a tall matching companion set, completed the picture. Nana had a type of iron square plate with two hooks which fitted over the front bars of the grate. I only learned many years later, it was to 'crisp up' a cooked joint of meat. However, needless to say, my Gran could not have afforded many joints of meat, but did make the most delicious toast on it! Above the fireplace was a large over mantle, the full width of the fireplace. In its centre was a large mirror, edged with mahogany small shelves leading off to both sides. The obligatory wooden clock took pride of place in the centre of the mantelpiece, with a large white spotted dog on each side. Nana always had a dark green velvet mantle cloth, ruffed at intervals, with dozens of small pom-poms running along its edges. Imagine my joy, one day, on discovering that if I pulled a tiny thread, I could unravel these little balls one after the other!! For this I was sent down below to our rooms in disgrace! Jutting from the wall on each side of the fireplace, two (once brass) tubular lengths held the old gas mantles in place. How I loved curling up in front of the glowing fire, listening to the hissing sound they made. When they 'dimmed', the old lady would put another penny in the meter and once again the room would be enveloped in a warm glow. The centre of the room was dominated by a huge, round, polished table, supported by a large column with several claw-like legs. A very tall lamp, its white glass globe showing a thick white wick, the middle a pink bulbous shape leading down into a brass stand, stood on the centre table. My next most favourite item was the biggest photo album I have ever seen. The cover, made of a thick embossed material, had a very large clasp holding it closed. As a child, it took my two small hands to turn a page. Here again one would suspect the past grand ladies of this once fine house had just stepped out and left it behind! Oh, those wonderful old sepia pictures, showing small waisted ladies in splendid gowns. And always the same question. 'Nana, is this you? Is this your Mammy?' and always the same reply, 'That's

148

Auntie Katie.' I never did learn who Aunt Katie was, not until I started researching my family, when I was almost as old as my beloved Nana! A huge sideboard stood in place on the wall opposite the fire place. It was so long, I wondered how they had managed to get it up the wooden spiral staircase of our old tenement house! As a child, I could not imagine it coming apart in sections! The polished top, with lace runner held three glass shades, one large one at each end, with a smaller one in the middle. The taller ones housed religious statues, while the centre one held an array of stuffed birds. A Jewish gentleman, a customer of my granddad, the shoemaker, was really eager to buy this piece of furniture, but the old lady would never sell it. Ma maintained it was made from mahogany. Every year, on Easter Sunday, all twelve grandchildren would gather and Nana would produce an array of Easter eggs from one of the three cupboards of the sideboard. These always consisted of boxed ones for the boys and little baskets for the girls. Our eyes almost popped out of our heads when she showed us the 'secret drawer' inside its cupboard! My vivid imagination knew no bounds, and, as the years passed, I convinced myself that my Nana was really a lady who, despite family objections, had married my poor granddad, a simple shoe maker. How else could one explain her beautiful manner of speech, her exquisite taste in clothes, her impeccable manners? Looking back, I now realize my Nana could not have afforded the nice clothes she wore. I can only think she obtained them from a lady she worked for. Even today, I can close my eyes and see this tiny doll like woman with finely chiselled features, beautiful, even in old age. My earliest recollection of my grandmother has her dressed in a black velvet hip length cloak, covered in a floral design of black jet beads, with a long black skirt just touching the top of tiny, buttoned boots. She always wore a bonnet and later a hat. She only ever wore black, that is apart from the black crossover pinafore decorated with tiny lavender flowers. Some years later, the beads of the cloak began to unravel and fall off.

I was given the cloak and together with my two little friends sat for hours on the back steps of our tenement house, where we unpicked all the tiny beads and spent endless happy hours threading them for necklaces and bracelets. Some time ago I managed a trip to Dublin, and quite by chance managed to get the phone number of one of my two little childhood friends. I made arrangements to visit and on arriving at her daughter's home found she was now suffering from dementia. We had not spoken for fifty five years! I was not even sure she remembered me, staring blankly at most of my, 'Do you remember?' Then, not only to mine, but also to her family's amazement she asked me, 'Do you remember your Nana's lovely beaded cloak, the one she gave you to play with? What fun and happy hours we had with it.' I've got to admit, I was oh, so sad, but proud.

Chapter Twenty Three
My Da, The John Wayne of Ireland

While life in the Dublin tenements was pretty grim, it did have its lighter side, as illustrated by the following true story. 'My Da The John Wayne of Ireland'. Dublin 1949. Looking at the beautiful O Connell Street, Dublin's main thoroughfare, with its exquisite hats, dresses, books and old worldly sweet shops, it would be hard to imagine the decrepit, crumbling, rat infested houses which lay a few hundred feet behind its fancy façade. And, as if to add insult to injury, the busy abattoir was placed squarely among us, much, I might add, to the joy of the local boys!! Known to us as, 'The slaughter House', they (the boys) would call there and, depending on the mood of the foreman, come away with the bladder of some dead animal. This would be stuffed with all sorts of material from newspapers, auld rags, to goodness knows what, resulting in a football which gave them many hours of pleasure, for as long as it lasted. Why this abattoir was situated here right in the centre of town remains a mystery. Perhaps the City Fathers thought its putrid smell might offend the sensibilities of our more affluent brothers and sisters living in the grand houses of the outer city! Even for us city children, it was not uncommon to see a herd of cows being driven towards the slaughter house. The drover or farmer would have walked many miles, from some outlying farm, to get them there. At the top of our street, but on the opposite side of the road, stood a very large factory, (Williams and Woods). It was so big it occupied almost the whole block. Employing many hundreds of people, it produced jams, boiled sweets, sauces and canned beans. It traded under the name of 'Chef'. Every day the sound of its huge hooter could be heard for miles around, as it heralded lunch break. Unfortunately, on one particular day, just as the farmer was herding his large herd past the factory, the hooter went off! This caused a stampede that would have done justice to a western picture. The terrified cattle ran in all directions, seeking ways of escape. They ran up the narrow entrance to the factory, blocking it as the poor auld farmer frantically tried to get them under control. A huge bullock, finding its way blocked, turned back, the whites of its eyes showing this poor animal's terror. Spying the open space of our street, it made for there, causing people to run in all directions to avoid getting crushed! Meanwhile, back at the ranch, (sorry) our house, we had just sat down to a hurried lunch when the most horrendous noise brought us to our feet! My poor Ma, white faced and blessing herself, truly thought the old house was falling down around her! Unknown to us, the huge bullock had entered our hall. (We never locked hall or room doors, none of us had anything worth stealing). It could not have picked a worse place to seek shelter; ours had the narrowest hall in the whole street! Already under a compulsory order for demolition, it felt as if the auld foundations had already given up the ghost! Ma would later remark, that was the only time she saw us leave the table with food still on our plates! We were up like lightning ready to make our great escape.' Jaysus,' I would muse years later, 'Steve Mc Queen had nothing on us lot! '. My Da was not in the best of form that day! He had returned early from the quay, after failing to get work on a boat and most likely did not even have the price of a woodbine. Ah, sure, let's dramatise this tale by describing how he heroically ventured off (four steps, kitchen to hall) on a reconnaissance mission to investigate the cause of this great commotion.

Opening the door, he came face to face with the bullock now lodged firmly in our very narrow hall. 'Jaysus!' He closed the door that fast it looked like one of those revolving doors ya see in the fancy shops! We were trapped. Lol! 'What's up?' was the question on everyone's lips, on eyeing the already large crowd of people vying for a better position outside our hall door? The cry went up, relayed from those nearest the door to the ring of outer spectators. 'There's a Bull in He-----y's hall.' Ah, sure we weren't used to excitement like this on a weekday, usually having to wait for Saturday night for that pleasure! 'The Battle of The Bull' had begun! It's objective, to get the bull out of the hall. It did not help matters that the auld fool, Bottler Kelly from next door who fancied himself as another Noel Purcell (my a-se), was playing to the crowd. Already, he had rushed home and returned with his kid's cowboy hat, throwing it through our now open window and telling dad to, 'Try that for size.' The wall separating us from this crazed animal was only a light wooden partition. Poor Ma, now frantically holding up her precious dresser (on our side of the wall), as every movement of this unwanted visitor to our home was sending contents crashing to the floor. The Child of Prague statue came hurtling across the room minus its head. That, the head, had gone missing months ago. I swear our Jem had nicked it, ground out the facial features and used it for a marble! Me granny's lovely silver (plated) teapot was the next to come flying, as we dived and ducked the flying objects. This (the teapot) was our 'family heirloom'. We proudly boasted to one and all of how our granny had nicked this from a jeweller's window in Henry Street during the troubles! According to our granny, the tans had come flying up Henry Street in a covered lorry, pulled up, and after throwing the cover aside, proceeded to open fire indiscriminately, causing mayhem and panic. Men, women and children dashed to take cover wherever they could find it. Our granny happened to be just outside the jewellery shop at the corner of the arcade facing Moore St. When the large window was shot through, she, like everyone else, helped herself! God, I wished she had been more selective in her choosing but, Jaysus love me auld granny, on reflection, she didn't have much choice with the Tans bullets flying all around her! For years we thought the auld teapot was the 'real thing', that was until me Ma tried to pledge it in Bretons pawnshop in Capel Street and Pat told her it wasn't worth the pot you'd piss in! So, as I was telling ya, before I got carried away with me poor auld granny God rests her soul. By now, the younger children were hysterical and clinging to Ma's apron. One sister showed her true colours by trying to escape (unsuccessfully) through the open front window, but changed her mind when she saw the drop of the cellar area she had to cross! Ma, still trying to keep her precious auld dresser upright, was furious as my older sister and myself were now on the floor doubled up laughing. 'Jaysus!' Her language was choice, I wasn't even aware me Ma knew words (censored) like that! Her frustration at not being able to get her hands on the pair of us did not help the situation! Under the circumstances, perhaps I should have refrained from asking, 'Shall we send for the cavalry'? and 'Think of the Alamo.' Now, that fell as flat as a pancake. And still the crowd gathered outside, well out of danger of the raging bull and now amusing themselves by offering helpful suggestions. 'Shoot the bastard and we'll all have steak tonight!' And, 'I'll have mine rare, but the mott likes hers well done'! 'Can ya throw a few onions in with the auld steak, only I'm partial to me onions!' The last remark from a snotty-nosed Bottler Kelly, causing our already fuming Da's hackles to rise even further. The laughter was soon wiped from the face of our Julia, with the proclamation from Da that he was going to take charge of the situation. He would now issue orders and suggestions to the drover on the other side of the partition that was our hall! Looking at her in horror I mouthed the words, 'For feck's sake, what does he know about cows?'. The way he

154

was going on, you'd think he had worked in the fecking rodeo all his life.

Apart from the few cows that passed the top of our street, on the way to the abattoir, the nearest my Da had been to a cow was at the Maro, our local flea pit. Me and our Julia was only mortified at the way Da was acting! In a matter of minutes and, in his mind, he had not only donned the (invisible) wild west attire, but I swear we could even detect a John Wayne drawl to his broad Dublin accent! Julia and I kept well out of sight of the onlookers outside, just in case some fellas we knew might be part of the crowd! We'd have died of embarrassment. Mind, in the event of that happening, we had made up our minds to disown our Da and say he was a poor auld eejit that lived in the 'two pair front' of our house. So, there we had it, a fecking half ton bullock lodged in our narrow hall with the poor auld farmer behind it trying to do the impossible, get it out on to the street. (Da, shouting to farmer on the other side of the partition.) 'Can ya hear me?' (Kerry accent with sob) 'I can sir, I can.' Da: 'Now, listen carefully. This is what I'm going to do. I'm going to leave the house through the back ground floor window, approach the animal from the back yard and try to pull it out to the back yard. I'll pull and you push! Have ya got that? Kerry accent, (still with sob) 'Ah, Jasus, the Lord save us I have, I have.' Oh Yeah!! The idea was to drive it out into the back yard, turn it around and drive it back on to the street. Had Da forgotten the poor beast would have to navigate the back stairs? Da left the house by the back window and went around to the back hall. On seeing movement in front of him, the already terrified animal charged forward, thus freeing itself from the narrow hall, but leaving the farmer flat on his face. A white faced Da, (no fool) seeing this several hundredweight of beef on the hoof coming towards him, took to his heels heading for our large back yard! He was now in our view as we had all rushed to the back window, waiting to see the bullock come into the yard. I had never seen him move so swiftly, in one

155

leap he reached the safety of the top of the wall causing my brother to remark, 'Remind me to enter him for the high jump, he'd fecking walk a gold medal.' Likewise, our neighbours had also rushed from the front to the back windows of their houses, thus having a bird's eye view over our back yard. So now we have a pasty-faced man astride a wall, and a bloody crazed bull running mad around our back yard. Thank God, while we may have had the narrowest hall in the street, we certainly had the biggest back yard. Ma, now calmer and feeling a bit safer from the safety of the back window, shouted, 'Mick, will you for God's sake get down off that wall and give the poor animal a drink of water. Do you think it would like some bread?' You will gather from this, Ma was a city girl through and through. I have to say, Da may have sworn at work, but seldom in front of us children. However, on this occasion, it would be wiser to take the Fifth Amendment than repeat his reply! Entering into the spirit of the situation yet again, the bold Bottler from next door started singing, 'Home, home on the range' and all our neighbours joined in, much to Dad's chagrin. Still sitting astride the wall he told them, 'Why don't some of you fecking smart arses come on in and show us what you can do'? Naturally, there were no takers. We may have been very poor in our street, but we certainly weren't daft. I can't remember who, but I think it was our Jem suggested from our window, 'Da, grab one of Ma's sheets from the line and do what them fellows in Spain do!' Eventually the drover, now in the yard, managed to turn the bullock and get it up the back stairs where it then rushed madly into the street. The crowds outside, not expecting this, had to drop bicycles and run in all directions. One young man nearest the door even leapt over the railings, falling into the deep basement area and breaking an ankle. I (still laughing) returned to work explaining I was several hours late, because I could not get out of the hall due to a bullock blocking it. 'Pull the other one,' said the foreman, 'do you expect me to believe that cock and bull story? You're suspended for two days.

Chapter Twenty Four
The Long Wait

Wouldn't it be wonderful, I mused, if to keep and hang on to our memories, we could bottle them up like pickles and preserve them for our lifetime, opening the jar at leisure and selecting the one we wanted to revisit and relive. Naturally, we would then have to have separate labels, deciding which memory went into which jar. Ah, but then again, perhaps not. The mind has its own way of assimilating memories, and dealing with the wounds of long forgotten slights, hurts and loss. We are lucky enough to live opposite a school and are blessed to be able to watch the little ones skip, hop and jump all the way from the school gate to the school door. I see mums and dads hurrying up the path for parent-teacher meetings, eager to learn what progress their little darlings are making. I am warmed and made happy, watching the togetherness of these lovely family units, as they deliver and collect their children to and from school each day. I see parents taking their children to the nearby farm to acquaint them with the animals. And yet, as I watch, unbidden and unsolicited, comes an 'if only'. I banish it swiftly from my mind, knowing that it will bring a sadness and heaviness to this old heart. Alas, the past persists in bleeding into the present, and reluctantly I sup from the cup of memory. I try to but cannot recall a single occasion when I went out with my mother, father and siblings, as a family. We seemed to go everywhere with our Ma. Of course, there were the few and far between times, when our Da would take us over to visit his mother on a Sunday morning. We would stand outside our hall door, faces scrubbed and shining, ribbons in place, waiting for Da

to finish shaving. Ma's dire warnings of, 'Get a mark on them socks and I'll kill ya stone dead,' went over our heads! How often had we heard that before? Our father would walk us all the way over to Oliver Bond flats, on the other side of the river. We kids felt like the cavalry trespassing on Indian Territory. How could I forget those visits? I will forever associate the smell of boiled cabbage with our paternal grandmother! She always insisted that
 we children drink a cup of the vile water, as she uttered the immortal words: 'All the goodness is in the cabbage water.' Da's mother was really nice. She was named Kitty, and she always gave us two pennies as we left her flat. I had no idea until the day I disobeyed Ma and she shouted, 'Go on now, just ya keep that up and I promise ya, your Da will leave you at home when we all go to Dollymount on Sunday.' I couldn't believe it. We were going out with both our parents! I was, like all little girls, proud of my Da and wanted to be seen out and about with him. Such a simple thing and yet a rarity, as far as mine and a few of the other fathers of my street were concerned. I was so proud! I made sure I dropped the forthcoming trip into the conversation every chance I got, in school and at play in the street. Casually winding a strand of hair around my finger, I gave a huge sigh to emphasize our family's (supposed) dilemma! As I explained to my friend Nancy. Well, me Da hasn't made up his mind yet but it's definitely between Dollymount and Portmarnock.' 'Ger off outa that! I don't believe ya, sure you're only boasting.' 'I am not! As a matter of fact (sigh,) we were all going to go down to the country but we couldn't leave me poor auld granny on her own for very long 'cause she's so old.' What perfectly behaved children we were in the week leading up to the seaside trip. We ran for the messages with never a murmur of, 'Ah Ma, send her, I went for the last one.' Finally, Sunday arrived and after we all got back from early Mass, Ma started the preparations for our day out.

Jaysus, not only brawn sandwiches but corned beef ones as well! Me mouth was only watering already. Our family then numbered six. The older ones were each given a bag containing enough equipment to see a troop of boy scouts through a jamboree. The boys carried an assortment of odd cups, towels, bottles of milk and lemonade, sandwiches, wrapped in the paper from a Boland's loaf, biscuits and, of course, a teapot. We were ready at last! Ma watched the clock as she waited for me Da who had 'just slipped out for one'. We all waited and waited, the younger ones becoming restless and impatient, until finally my eldest brother was sent to 'The Beamish' to see what was keeping me Da. He returned saying, 'Da said we are to go on out to Dollymount and he will follow us.' I could see first anger and then disappointment etched on my mother's face. Ma and her six children set off to catch the bus to Dollymount, weighed down by an assortment of bags. Alighting from the bus, we walked along the road leading to the beach. The right hand side consisted of huge boulders leading to the water's edge. Families never used that side of the beech. We passed the woman who sold boiling water for making tea. Even standing yards away, the heat from the fire under the very large water container could be felt, making our already sun kissed faces even redder. For a small deposit, one could even hire the teapot with the boiling water, but you supplied your own loose tea; no teabags in those days! We saved a few pence by boiling our own water. It was not a particularly clean beach and even before we staked our claim to a small part of it, we had to clear it of an accumulation of rubbish, left behind by earlier sun worshippers. Our first job, on arriving, was to collect enough kindling to make a fire ready for our tea later in the day. We children undressed, the small girls young enough just to wear knickers, while we older ones wore vest and knickers. We did not possess bathing costumes. How we loved splashing in and out of the water, trying to outrun yet another large wave, as it headed inwards toward the beach.

160

Ma's cries of, 'Don't go out too far,' or 'Hold the hands of the younger ones,' went unheeded. We were too busy enjoying our rare treat out. The older lads were trying to grab us to duck us under the water. 'You two better feckin' give over or I'll tell me Ma,' I threatened, not that they took much notice! I turned, ready to shout and complain to my Ma. She was some distance away. I held my hands to my eyes as a shield against the sun, seeking out and finding her solitary figure surrounded by all the bags and discarded clothes. She looked so alone. Like me, she too had her hands to her eyes, her head, still turned to the direction of the top road, still waiting for my Da's arrival, but he never came. I felt a pain, not like the pain I felt when I fell and cut my knee, but something sharp in my chest that made me want to rush to my mother and say, 'It's alright Ma, we're here.' Even at that young age, I felt my mother's loneliness. Inwardly, I raged against my Da and his cronies in 'The Beamish'. I wanted to cry for her. I left the water and ran to join her. Later, the two older boys would get the fire started amidst much puffing and blowing and Ma made the tea, when the water finally boiled. Nothing tasted as good as those sandwiches, despite the grains of sand that had somehow found their way between the thick slices of turnover. It was as if a swarm of locusts had descended upon our group! In less than half an hour there wasn't a crumb left. The large bag of broken biscuits from Miss. O'Toole's shop was, to us children, an added luxury. When we had excitedly gone into the shop for the biscuits, she had even cut off two slices of gur cake and given them to our youngest children. Miss O'Toole was one of the kindest people in our community. She played a big part in the Children's lives, charting our way from a slice of gur cake to 'a penny Woodbine and a match please'. My father was a good man. We never went hungry. He worked hard when he could get the work but, like a lot of men of that era, felt that once the housekeeping money was handed up, there ended his responsibility. All those added expenses for occasions like Communion and

Confirmation, 'Ah well, sure the Ma could take care of that.'
I would not have been aware then that my mother would
receive no extra money for such occasions.
Ma would get clothes dockets for Bulger's, or I think
Cassidy's, from whence she would get the required clothes.
It meant she would have just paid off one lot, when yet
another child was due to be confirmed and the whole
process would start all over again. Even as a child, I
jealously wondered how come Uncle Frank took his
children off every Sunday. He would take them all over the
city, pointing out places of interest, relating stories of the
part different buildings had played in the troubled history of
our city. This, from a man who worked six nights a week
and yet, would and did, give up his one free day to his
family! Why, I asked could my Da not take us out like that?
I have, in other 'Recollections', touched upon the part, or
lack of it, played by some of the fathers in the tenements. I
do not doubt for a moment that they would have stood up to
the Devil himself to protect their families, but yet, sadly, I
believe they always held back in the showing of that most
important emotion, love. Maybe not in the giving, but
certainly in the expression of it. In their misguided belief, I
think that they saw it as a sign of weakness. They saw how
the very few other men in our area were ridiculed for
playing an active part in family life, the latter referred to as
Mollies or Mary Ann's. Was not the rearing of children
women's work? They would never even attempt to push a
pram, someone might see them! My father belonged to the
latter category. Ah, if I was a fairy godmother, I would not
have hesitated in tapping some of the men of our street with
the wand of tactility! In old age, my Da would redeem
himself, not only with his own grandchildren, but all the
children living around. It is hard to believe mothers, who
could not get their children to eat, would bring them to our
house asking for my father's help. The child would be sat at
our table and Da, with a never ending depth of patience,
would cajole, coax, and finally 'aeroplane' the food into a

162

now giggling tot's mouth. Mind you, I think my Ma's cooking contributed towards the child's appetite. It pleased me that our children discovered a grandfather who found the time to play and listen to them. I am sad that during my lifetime, or should I say my father's life time, not once did I ever hear him say, 'Ah, you're Da loves ya.' I will go to my grave wondering, why?

Chapter Twenty Five
The Cleaning Ladies

'But Ma, how did I know you only said it in temper?' asked my fourteen year old brother Jem, as he looked at our Ma's astonished face. 'Sure, you'll have to go now. Mr Brady the office manager said to tell me Ma to come in for an interview tomorrow at 10 o'clock.' It was only the previous day, when the whole gang of us were driving Ma around the bend, that she had uttered the immortal words,'Jaysus, I'd rather go out and scrub floors than put up with you lot any longer. At least I'd have a few hours peace away from the lot of ya.' Jem, who worked as a messenger boy for a firm of film distributors just a few doors up from the Corinthian cinema on the quays, had taken Ma at her word and inquired about the cleaner's job that was being advertised. Ma had never worked from before she was married, having a large family to look after. The next morning saw our nervous mother being interviewed and accepted for the cleaner's job. The hours were from 6.00 to 8.00 every evening, and 7.00 to 8.00 each morning. The offices consisted of two adjoining houses, one house for the typists and other clerical workers, while the interlinking house (number two) was for the directors and owners of the business. While each house had three storeys, the top floors were never used. Of course, lots of changes had to take place now that Ma had accepted the job. We older girls had to see to the younger children who were not a problem, as they were not babies. There was far too much work for one woman and the trouble was my Ma was very particular about cleaning. She cleaned those offices, as she would her own home, putting everything into it. There were no mops about in those days, it was all down on your hands and knees, scrubbing and polishing. House number 1 was the hardest to do, having lino everywhere which had to be scrubbed and polished. House 2 was fully carpeted, apart from the toilets, so that was easier to clean. Sometimes, our Ma could hardly walk home she was so tired. Not only was she looking after her own large family, but also her mother and father who lived with us. She was not a big robust woman. She would spend about ten years in this job. My sisters had the bright idea of going along and helping our mother with the evening cleaning, but she would not hear of it, terrified she'd get the sack if she was found to have unauthorised people in the office! 'Ma, they will all have gone home, how will they know who's in the office? And there's feck all in there to steal. Sure, we're hardly going to walk out of there with a couple of typewriters under our arms, are we?' And so, we managed to persuade Ma to let us help. The only problem with this was if Ma heard someone coming back up the stairs for a forgotten umbrella, or an item left behind, she would hurry us into the small room that held the stationary. We would stay there as quite as mice until given the all clear! Kevin always found an excuse to return to the office on the pretext of having left some important papers behind. The truth was he was a lonely young man of about 30ish who lived with his aged mother, and would use any excuse to avoid going home, according to the gossipy typist in house number one. Apparently, while he was a genius with figures (alas, the ones on paper), he was a very shy, young man who hardly ever went out with people his own age and had never had a girlfriend. The gossipy typist who my sisters and I had renamed 'Gobby' had given us the low down on Kevin, but in a sneering way. This was after we were accepted as Ma's helpers. Kevin liked talking to our mother. She made him laugh, but he could never make out if she was just joking or serious, with some of the things she came out with!

It would take him years before he got used to her ways and would eventually join in with the banter. While we hid in what was no more than a cupboard, trying to suppress the laughter as we listened to our Ma trying to get rid of Kevin! 'Kevin, ya want to gather up yer papers and get off now, or you'll miss your bus.' 'Ah, no problem, Mrs. H. Sure, I'm on the auld bike today.' 'I wouldn't delay if I were you, look at them dark clouds, it's going to pour down.' This caused us to double over with laughter, ramming our fists into our mouths, so Kevin wouldn't hear us. Had Ma forgotten, the blinds were all drawn? 'Ah, I'm sure your Ma must be waiting for you to get home Kevin. Sure, she'll be going mad for a cup of tea, the poor soul.' 'Ah no, my Auntie Concepta calls in to make sure she's all right.' Kevin's mother had gone into hospital for surgery, and sadly had to have her left leg removed and two toes from her right foot. She was confined to a wheelchair. 'And tell me Kevin, how is your mother keeping these days?' 'She's doing really well; the doctors are very pleased with her.' 'Ah, God bless her. Sure, she's a walking miracle. This was too much! The straw that broke the camel's back! We fell out of the cupboard laughing, and our mother had no choice but to explain to a startled Kevin who we were and what we were doing there. 'Ah, sure that's grand, ' said Kevin. 'Your secrets safe with me.' He stood looking at us, his face getting redder by the minute. While he would have the banter with our Ma, it took him years before he really felt relaxed enough to talk with us. Two of us girls would go and one, usually my older sister, would set to with Ma in the first house, as it required the most cleaning. I would go to the second house, which was all vacuuming and polishing. I loved going into the director's office, as it had the largest bay window I had ever seen. It looked out onto the quays, the lights from the shops and cinema reflecting on the water, giving it an almost fairyland appearance. I would watch the people at the bus stops on wet, windy nights, pulling coat collars up closer around their necks and peering into the darkness for long overdue buses. I could almost see into the amusement arcade on the opposite side of the water. No matter which way you looked, from this window one had a grand view of the bustling quays. It was in this office that I made my wonderful discovery! While dusting a rather large cabinet, I accidentally sent hundreds of papers flying to the floor. On bending to pick them up, I found out they were very large glossy photographs of every major Hollywood star! To this teenager, it was like winning the pools! Why, it had taken Nancy and myself two years to get a little picture of Alan Ladd. Mind ya, we had put third class stamps on our request letters! I'll never forget that day we had arrived home from school and my Ma had asked, 'In the name of the Lord God, who do you know in America?' We had long given up hope of ever hearing from Alan Ladd! Dear God! I was in seventh heaven! Lying on my tummy, I snuggled even deeper into Mr. Elliman's deep white carpet, as I went through the pictures one by one: Clark Gable, Rita Haywood, Judy Garland, Jeff Chandler, Esther Williams, they were all there. I anxiously searched for my now favourite, Glen Ford. I had outgrown Alan Ladd, having been told he had to stand on a box to kiss the girl in the picture, because he was so small! God, I was in a world of my own; forgetting time, cleaning and everything else. All I wanted to do was go through every one of the hundreds of pictures I had discovered, which I eventually did over a long period, as there were so many. I even wondered should I take Glen Ford's photo home with me. I could smuggle it home in me knickers. The thought of it being missed and Ma losing her job swiftly put that idea out of me head! My sisters voice shouting up the stairs, 'Are ya finished?' brought me back from my dreams of Hollywood mansions, swimming pools and handsome young men with a quizzically raised eyebrow, inquiring, 'Would you care for a cocktail?' 'What's keeping ya?' 'Well, I think Mr. Elliman must have had a party to-day, ' I lied. 'Sure, the place is in a right state. Give me another half hour.' I worked like mad to make sure it was in order before Ma's arrival in the morning. I could never understand why she had to go back in the mornings. Sure, wasn't the whole place done? I think it was to turn on the lights and heating. Maybe they expected her to spread the work out over morning and evening. I did not let my sister know of my find, hugging this wonderful secret to myself and making sure when I went each evening, I got to do house number two. I have to admit I was reluctant to help out with the office cleaning, but what with the view from the window and picture discovery in the director's room, I almost ran to do the work each evening, much to the amazement of my Ma and my sister. I swear when I entered that room, it was like being transported to another world. Soft white drapes and deep white carpets was something I had never known, apart from what I had seen on the pictures, of course. How I loved the smell of the leather from the deep burgundy coloured chesterfield suite. After weeks of looking at the pictures, I turned my attention to the desk. It was huge with a beautiful green, leather top, with a blotting paper holder done in matching green leather. I came to the conclusion the boss did not do much work, as there was never a blot on the paper! It also held a box of Mr Elliman's favourite cigars. I would sit in his swivel chair, with my feet on the desk and my thumbs tucked into imaginary braces, just as I saw them do in the pictures. By now I was smoking the odd Woodbine and, eyeing the beautiful wooden cigar box, wondered, should I? Dare I? I did, and not only that, but also poured myself a measure of whiskey from the beautiful decanter, despite never having even tasted it before. I honestly felt like one of those hard-hitting newspaper hacks seen in the American pictures! I even played at being Sam Goldwyn, hiring and firing would be starlets, whiskey in one hand and cigar in the other! 'Don't call us, we'll call you.' And to my imaginary secretary, 'Ruthie, babe, send in the next one.' My need was more for the 'props' rather than the vile taste of both the cigar and the whiskey. Of course, that was the evening my Ma came to the other part of the house, only to find me with my head down the loo, not only bringing up the whiskey, but also my four previous meals! I think what really upset her was the thick pall of cigar smoke that lingered, not only over that office, but the outer offices as well. Poor Ma, she was almost crying, as with a newspaper she endeavoured to clear the smoke out of the windows she had already opened. Ye Gods, I never heard the end of it! I had dared to sully Mr. Elliman's office with smoke and, not only that, but had the audacity to pour a drink from his decanter! I could not help wondering if Mr Elliman wandered off down along the quays every time he wanted a smoke, rather than pollute his beautiful office? I doubt that. When I was finally allowed back to help with the cleaning, it was in house one and under the watchful eyes of Ma. In time our Ma, bless her, became a sort of agony aunt, the young typists seeking her advice on matters of the heart! She was possessed of such a dry wit and sometimes, on being asked by some lovelorn young typist, 'What should I do?' her usual advice would be to, 'run like hell.' The office had a lot of young men sent up from rural parts to start their career in the Dublin branch. My mother always felt so sorry for them, as in her own words, 'Sure, God love them and they so far from home and missing their Mas' Once we heard the words, 'Sit down there now, I have something to ask you.' We, by now teenagers, were always wary. 'You know that young lad I told you about, the one from Cork, you know the one I mean, the new lad in the office.' 'Well yeah, what about him?' 'Ah, God love him. Sure, he doesn't know a sinner in Dublin and can't even find his way around.' 'So, Ma, what do ya want us to do?' 'Well, could ya not see your way to going out on a date with the poor lad?' 'A Jaysus Ma! Ya want us to go out with a culshie with 28inch trouser bottoms! No way, and anyhow we have fellas of our own.' If she really pushed it, pulling at our heart strings with exaggerated tales of poor lads, far from home and sitting in auld digs missing their families, we did go out with 'the poor lost soul' on a couple of occasions, but always making sure we did not go to our regular dance halls for fear of bumping into our friends! Sure, it would all be over town in no time, if you were seen with a lad from Cork or Kerry! God how I hated when they took us to Barry's! For feck sake, what did I know about the 'Walls of Limerick'? Oh, what shallow young wans we were!

Every Friday, (pay day) as a reward for helping her out with the office cleaning, Ma took us into Cafola's in O'Connell Street and treated us to a 'melancholy baby'. Oh! The pure joy of sitting there, trying to make the ice-cream last for ages, reaching down with the long spoon trying to scrape every vestige from the glasses narrow bottom! Ma stayed in her office cleaning job for many years, until she left Dublin. She never worked again.

Chapter Twenty Six
Bang-Bang

More years ago than I care to remember we had several tramps in our fair city. We had "Johnny Forty Coats" so called because he wore several overcoats winter or summer. Another was "The Guard" because of his military bearing. Now he really was a handsome man beneath all the hair and grime. Standing 6ft 5ins. it was said he came home from the war a broken man and despite having a wealthy family elected to live on the streets. Everyone's favourite was a man named Silver or Bang- Bang. A fanatic for cowboy movies, the name Silver most likely came from "Hi ho Silver" (Lone Ranger) Bang- Bang always carried a large key of the old fashioned type, using it as a gun. If one was unlucky enough to get close to him he would dig you in the ribs with this key shouting "Bang, bang, Gotcha, your dead" Most of us would clutch the part where the "bullet" had entered and pretend to die on the spot!!! He would use the city buses as his "stage coach" hanging on to the rail as he took aim and shot the "baddies" He was a part of our city, known and loved by all, and everyone just played along and humoured him, (were we crazy or what?) Folk still talk of the day a bus load of American tourists arrived in the City centre. They must have thought they had been dropped off in Bedlam! Imagine the sight that greeted them. Bang-bang, ragged coat flying in the wind, unkempt silver hair all over the place shooting up the whole of town while children (and adults) shot back from doorways and any other place they could find to take cover! Imagine the surprise of the locals when the Americans joined in, shooting from behind pillar boxes and buses with cries of "Give up bub, your outnumbered" I often wondered did they think it was some sort of quaint local custom and they would fall in with it? You could not visit our city without meeting Bang-bang if he was out and about, part of the guided tour! Famous and immortalised in song Her poets they were many. Her writers they were plenty. There was Swift with all his little folk And Joyce and Molly Bloom. Her characters an unsung gang. There's "Forty Coats" and old "Bang, Bang"And "Zozimus" who always sang of dear old Dublin town I had long left home when my sister wrote to tell me of Bang-bang's death. How sad I was. Our city and its people had grown up with this character and his weird and wonderful ways. He was as familiar to us as our local monuments, so much so that his death was front page news. On the morning of his funeral, people lined the city streets in their thousands to pay their last respects to him.

The mourning coach was escorted by six police outriders and followed by city dignitaries and the people who had known and loved him. I believe the city fathers paid for his headstone. I promise myself I will go and visit his grave, not only to pay my respects but, hopefully to find out the real name of the man they called, Bang-bang.

Chapter Twenty Seven
Tough Times

Before I relate the story about my Da and his wooden leg, I would have to fill you in a little on his background. Perhaps the thing I admired most about him was his capacity for work. Having no "Trade" to fall back on he was reduced to taking casual work where ever and whenever he could get it. This work consisted mainly of labouring on the docks in the port of Dublin. He would go out early every morning, hail rain or snow in the hope of getting a days work. I have known him take on work other men refused, for instance an "ore" boat, when he would come home in the evening black as soot with his two eyes red and raw from the dust of this substance. Apparently, there were no health and safety regulations in those days (1940s) It became so difficult to get work that he later joined the British Army, eventually rising to the rank of sergeant. I can't remember if my mum went every Monday or once a month to collect the pension my da had allowed her, it was small but it was regular. Our family consisted of four boys and four girls. Michael, my eldest brother was a brilliant scholar and accepted for college but because my mum could not afford the cost of books or uniform his dream unfortunately passed him by. Not long afterwards he would die at the age of 16 years a tragedy my beloved mum never really got over, even into old age. My father was in Italy at this time and could not get compassionate leave. As well as bringing up eight children on her own my mum also looked after her aged parents, my Nan and granddad who lived with us. Times were so hard, not just for our family but also for those all around us. Bless her, my mum never lost faith and if we inquired "What are we going to do?" always came the same answer, God is good, something will turn up" and sure enough it did!! The "Gas Man "would turn up the following day to empty the meter and mum would get a rebate! We were so poor mum could not afford a headstone for her beloved first born Michael. She managed to stint and save enough to have a little wooden cross and rails made by a carpenter who lived in our street. It bore Michael's name and age but sadly was no match for the unpredictable weather and in time it too disintegrated as had her dreams for her darling boy. She would visit his grave every Sunday for her remaining years in Ireland. After the war, my father returned home, not only his good self but with all the discipline and regulations of army life! As we children left for church on Sunday morning he would stand at the door as we filed past him while he examined our nails to see they were clean and that our shoes well polished! He would not allow us girls to wear a headscarf which was all the fashion then, we had to wear hats. As soon as we turned the corner out would come the head-scarfs from under our coats and the hated hats hidden in their place. The boys were good sports and never "ratted" on us. My dad used the old "spit and polish" on his shoes every evening and even if it was snowing outside would not leave the house unless his shoes were shining. Our lovely mum was as soft as my dad was strict. She would threaten all sorts but never carry it out. If she thought my dad was going too far with us she would not hesitate in telling him "You're not in the Army now" From an early age I have always remembered the banging on the door of our tenement house at all times, mostly nights. Mum would go to answer and we would hear whispers of "She's due any time now, can you come" or sometimes "He/she has gone, the Lord have mercy on them" Mum would dress and then reach up for that mysterious brown box on top of the wardrobe and sail off into the night.

While understanding the latter, (someone had died and mum was called out to wash and lay them out) "she's due now" was still a mystery to us! We four girls, sharing the one bed would hazard a guess as to who was due now? Was some rich aunt coming from America? I secretly hoped so then we might get some proper blankets instead of this old army great coat we had on the bed for extra warmth! They could have at least removed the brass buttons! (I was 12 before I realized the "Queens Own Regiment" on my bottom was not a birthmark but the imprint of those blasted buttons) Of course our dreams of the rich American aunt melted like snow when an older playmate informed us it meant someone was having a baby! That mysterious box contained baby gowns, nappies, shawls and such like. You have to understand people were so poor they could not afford such items. My mum always kept them ready and loaned them until the child outgrew them. She would then take them back, wash and iron them ready for the next birth in our street of tenement houses.

Chapter Twenty Eight
Black Crepe Ribbons

As a child I can't recall having a fear of death or bodies laid out. As soon as we, the children of the street saw the small white card attached to the black crepe ribbon pinned to the hall door, we would make our way to the room of the bereaved. We would follow the actions of our elders using the small white feather set aside for that purpose to "bless" the corpse with holy water! I have to admit we were very liberal with the latter and, if there happened to be a few of us kids the bed would be swimming in holy water before we finished. Again, imitating our elders we would offer sympathies to the family of the deceased saying, "I'm sorry for your troubles". My God! We must have been strange children! If for some reason we were bored, and had nothing to do, (seldom) we would ramble around all the neighbouring streets looking for a tenement door with the familiar black crepe ribbon. In we would go and go through the same proceedings, even though we did not have a clue who the dead person was! We were never disappointed with the Union (Saint Kevin's Hospital") as there were always at least a couple of poor auld ones or auld fellows laid out in the dead house there. It was not unusual to see a couple of old pennies placed on their eyes to keep them closed. We all agreed it was very distressing to find a child laid out. When this happened we said extra prayers and, sometimes a whole rosary! When a funeral took place in our street it was a cause for great excitement for the young boys of the neighbourhood. In those far off days there were no lines of cars or mourning coaches. A hackney cab, pulled by some old horse was the means of transport to the cemetery. The streets boys would run along the long line of cabs begging the driver to allow them to sit up on the "Dickey" the seat adjacent to the driver. It may have been the custom as I never saw a cab driver refuse, well, that is except for one occasion! Unaware that it was only boys who were afforded this privilege, this small tom boy also ran along the line beaching each driver, "Please mister, will ya let me sit on you're dickey!" Ah, even to day I am reminded of the mortification mapped on the faces of my two brothers as they dragged me screaming and crying to our hall door where they locked me in!! From behind our "parlour" window and my Ma's lovely white lace curtains I sobbed as I watched the long line of cabs and listened to the sound of the clip clop of many horses as they turned the corner out of view. We young ones became adept at judging the popularity of the deceased by gauging how many glass shades covered the coffin lid and filled the hearse! I can't remember seeing fresh flowers; I think that would come years later. Of course the topic of conversation for days later would be the funeral. The street's gossips would have a field day assessing the coffin, the quality of the sandwiches and who wore what! "Ah, Biddy, did ya see it? It was only a gorgeous mahogany coffin with them lovely brass handles" "Mahogany! Mahogany me arse! I think they fecked off down to Noyke's and asked them to bang an auld box together! Hmmm, the mean bastards they didn't spend much on the poor auld fella considering they had him well backed! Mind ya, you mark my word Josie, their day will come, (sniff) Ah, Biddy, sure ya shouldn't be talking like that and the poor auld soul not even cold in his grave. Well, Josie, let me put it this way, if the poor auld fecker was depending on them sandwiches they served up he'd have died months ago. There wasn't two ounces of corned beef on the whole plateful of bread and, as for the so called coddle! I've put more in the slop bucket to feed Paddy Heffernan's pigs. Ah, Biddy! Ya should be showing some respect at a time like this. Me!

177

Show respect! Now if ya want to talk about respect Josie, lets talk about yer one that came over from England for the funeral. That dress was cut that low her diddies were almost hitting the corpses face as she bent over to kiss him goodbye. Sniff, did ya notice her wedding ring looked very new considering she was supposed to have married yer man years ago! That fecking family are as deep as the ocean, they only tell ya what they want ya want to know! To day I shudder at the macabre interest we children showed in viewing dead people. When I tell my own children of this practice of long ago they shake their heads in astonishment!

Chapter Twenty Nine
Dublin Pubs & Auld Mugs

As soon as one opened the door of the pub the nostrils were assailed by the smell of tobacco, beer, and indeed urine from the open door of the men's toilets. There were no women's toilets in the pubs at that time. I myself have seen old women come outside the pub, stand above the gratings normally used to lower the barrels and pee away! It was to be hoped the cellar man was not clearing the area when this occurred! The room was long and the polished counter, its top stained with the ring marks of the many pint glasses, followed the shape of the room culminating at its end in what was known as the "snug". A brass foot rail on which the men rested a foot as they leaned on the counter and drank numerous pints of beer was a stark contrast to the saw dust covered floor. The wall behind the bar was covered by large mirrors proclaiming in large print how "Guinness was good for you" and "Jameson's whiskey was smooth to the taste" In the Dublin of the 1940/50s, the pubs (bars) really were bastions of male supremacy where the men socialised, most of them spending money they could ill afford while the mammy stayed at home fretting about how she was going to make ends meet. This Holy Grail was forbidden to women with the exception of the "Auld ones" as the streets grannies were affectionately known!! Even then the auld ones were assigned to the snug, usually a small narrow room that would seat about ten. This retreat was partitioned from the main room by a wall of wood and frosted glass which did not reach the ceiling thus giving them access to the swearing, fights, and conversations taking place in the main room. Apart from the grannies, women did not enter pubs. I wondered were the auld ones afforded this privilege because they had reached the later years of their lives and, as many were widows and had no man to answer to? The snug was where they gathered in their uniform of black fringed shawls covering the cross-over aprons and stout black shoes/boots. They would linger over their bottles of Guinness or, depending on funds or the generosity of a son in the main bar a small "Baby power" they would talk of the old days, their families and the latest gossip of the street. The grannies of Dublin played a huge part in its social structures. They were the ones who, having raised a large family of their own willingly took on the added responsibility of grandchildren, taking them to live with them in the many cases of overcrowding of their own offspring's dwellings. This was such a common practice that sometimes we children addressed the children with the grannies surname. Overcrowding amongst families in the tenement rooms was a major problem especially when the children became teenagers.

Grown up children could no longer be expected to share a bedroom and this is where most grannies came into their own taking as many as three boys or girls to live with them. Even meal times brought its own problems and the only solution was to feed the families separately which involved more stratagems than would be necessary in organising a Saint Patrick's parade! Grannies were highly respected by their children and grandchildren. They would get away with almost anything and indeed there were those who shamelessly revelled in the role of matriarch. The auld ones were the ones called upon to sort out most of the problems which, if they could, they invariably did but with one exception. If a daughter or son wanted to return home due to martial problems the auld one was adamant in her refusal. It was almost like a mantra, "You made your bed,

now lie on it" and under no circumstances would they allow a son or daughter back home whatever the justification.
I write of a time when divorce was unheard of, a time when even a separation would bring great shame on the family. They, the older generation were of a school who believed that when you married, it was for life whatever the pitfalls or circumstances. Sadly, the full breakdown of conventional gender role was still a very far off distant dream for many of the women who suffered obscene brutality at the hands of drunken husbands The expression, Macho Man" had not even entered our vocabulary way back then, had it done, I reckon the men in and around our area would have won first prize in the stakes for the title. As most of the men were Dockers, with the reputation for being a hard tough lot, to be seen pushing a pram, or indeed doing any type of "woman's work" was unheard of, they would never have lived it down. It was considered unmasculine to look after children. I am perhaps being unfair here to the very few men who were brave enough to defy convention and help their wives. Looking back now, with hindsight, I applaud those men who had enough courage and compassion to recognise what a hard lot their women had to put up with and got on with the job of doing their bit even if in most cases it was behind closed doors. They suffered the jibes and derision of their neighbours and were referred to locally as Molly/Mary Anns. Of course I was not even aware of such matters then. For me and many others, the sight of men coming home very drunk and beating up their wives was the norm, something one got used to in our tenement environment. In fact I am loath to say these, usually Saturday night fights between spouses became a form of diversion for the women of the street after their mundane day of washing, cooking and cleaning, something that broke the monotony and took them away from, (sad to say,) their own worries and problems. As soon as a fight broke out up would go the cry "Ruggy up, Ruggy up. the call sign to say a fight had broken out or was in progress. No peeking from

181

behind curtains here! Every window in the street would be thrown open and propped up with some suitable object, a pillow or cushion placed on the hard outside window ledge and only then would the tenant kneel on the floor, elbows placed on the cushion for comfort lean out to get a better view! During a lull in the fight, the wife or husband might catch sight of the "spectators" and would angrily shout "What are you lot looking at? Have ya had a good look now?" peppered with many expletives causing every cushion/pillow to be hastily withdrawn and the windows closed in record time. The strange thing was nobody interfered or tried to pacify or ease the situation, not even family members! If on the rare occasion someone would try to break the row up they would be the ones to come out of it the worse for wear! There appeared to be an unwritten law, you don't interfere even if at that point the woman or man involved in the fight was covered in blood and in need of medical attention. In the end the granny of the family was always called upon to ease the situation and because, as stated they were respected she was the one who could (using the sharp end of her tongue) bring the altercation to a close. I think the secret was no one could turn around and berate a granny as this would not be tolerated by any of the streets inhabitants, they were to be shown respect at all times no matter what the situation. I would be about sixteen years of age before I really began to notice and question the injustices that were happening all around me. Already two years into working and having learned the "Facts of life" from older girls/women in the factories where I worked, albeit second hand, this simple mind could not equate or come to terms with the inequality and injustices which I was beginning to notice. I was not educated or old enough to see the picture as a whole, had I been, I think I would have been first on the queue to join the suffragettes.

Chapter Thirty
Louie

Before I start writing this information on my sister Julia Murphy who is a patient in Moorside I wish to make it clear the following contents can only be used for the express purpose of trying to determine if any of the following events or happenings contributed to her present condition. While I mention "events" and "happenings" on reflection my sister Julia lead what would appear in this day and age a rather uneventful life. Of course you will appreciate because of her age, what is considered the norm or acceptable now was unacceptable in the era we were brought up in! Where do I start? How does one write about a beloved sister in an unbiased way? If I am honest, I am not sure what information is exactly required so shall just reflect on her life as I remember it. We were all brought up in a very poor part of Dublin of working class parents. What we lacked in material things was more than compensated for in the abundance of love shown by our parents and grandparents who lived with us. While our father was a strict disciplinarian our mother was the complete opposite. Although my sister was named "Julia" when she was born in 1932 she would be forever known by the family as "Louie" Our faith as Roman Catholics was an important part of our upbringing and still is to this day, the latter of course from choice. Our childhood was similar to that of all the children in our neighbourhood, street games, school, and cinema and so forth. Our family consisted of four boys and four girls. Our oldest brother died at the age of sixteen years. While some family members were very clever and had the ability to go on to further education this was denied them due to lack of funds. In those days there was no government help with books and uniforms so on reaching the age of 14 years we just left school and went to work to supplement the family income. Julia could not wait to leave school and go to work! I can't say she enjoyed her school years! While the other three girls settled into mundane jobs as sewing machinists she flitted into about three jobs before settling down. I am not embarrassed in saying she was strikingly beautiful with an abundance of natural auburn curly hair and she was not even aware of how good looking she was! As a teenager Julia was not into sports or dancing as were her sisters. She loved live shows and the cinema. Her great passion was clothes and looking nice something she pursued up until the time of her illness. Sadly, while she could have had the pick of any young men the young man she eventually married was not a good choice. Let's just say he formed a very good relationship with alcohol! By now she was the mother of two young boys and finally a much longed for baby girl, Kathleen. In 1952/3 a flu epidemic was rife in Ireland claiming many lives. Julia was admitted to hospital with pneumonia and the baby Kathleen to a children's hospital with the dreaded flu. Sadly, Kathleen died, she was aged eighteen months. Julia was heartbroken but had tremendous support from our parents during this sad time. She and her husband then decided to move to England with the boys to make a fresh start. Again on arrival in Manchester they received support from family members until they got themselves established. The boys settled in well and made friends with their cousins already living here. The marriage went from bad to worse until eventually they split up. The husband went to live in another part of England and did not have any input in the boy's lives financially or otherwise. Julia went out to work to support her boys. Our parents had by this time also moved to Manchester from Ireland where nearly all of their children were now living.

They played a major part in bringing up the two boys. After many years Julia formed a friendship with another man. It was not a "live in" relationship as they each had their own flat. By now the two boys (young men) had immigrated to Australia and she was very lonely. She really missed her "boys" She went out to visit them in Australia and on her return faced the horror of finding this chap dead in her flat where he had gone to prepare things for her homecoming. He had died of a heart attack and was dead for several days. I can't begin to imagine what effect this had on her. She is not a strong person who can take control of a situation but then who would not go to pieces when faced with something like this? I have to be honest and say she is a born "worrier" meeting and worrying about events before they even happen! Despite reassurance and having her problems sorted by others she will still worry about very minute things! I should mention she is fanatical about her home and cleanliness. The valance on the bed must just "touch" the floor!!! If it is too short or too long it would not do, it had to be removed and adjusted (usually by one of her sisters as she does "not do" sewing, bless her! Had I not loved her so much I would have been jealous at the amount of people who would stop to tell me they had seen my sister Julia and how glamorous and lovely she always looked when they met her out shopping? It made me very proud. How it saddens me to see her as she is today a shadow of the once vibrant well groomed lady who took such pride in her appearance. Julia had a great capacity for making friends and was very popular. I was always amazed at her commitment to her friends and their loyalty to her. Even people she had met casually on holiday would keep in touch by letter or phone and were never just "Ships that passed in the night" She is one of the most thoughtful and generous people I know. Of course she was not perfect! Like everyone else she has her Achilles heel! If she wanted something she could be demanding and keep on and on until she got it! Vincent and Julia had worked at the same firm for many years. With a few other really nice people they had formed a small clique that all got on really well together. After the death of Vincent's wife they started to go out socially. They were good for each other, two lonely middle aged people whose families had both flown the nest. Our family were so happy that she had met someone who, it was apparent loved her deeply. Vincent moved in with Julia and they both enjoyed the same things which was an added bonus. They went through a bad patch when Vincent was diagnosed with cancer. She worried and fretted visiting him daily in the hospital. They really looked out for each other. Thankfully, Vincent recovered but then, tragically lost his son. He is a man of immense courage and fortitude as has been seen through past events and during Julia's long illness. I ask myself, how many times has he felt like giving up? For Vincent, there is always a light at the end of the tunnel. Up until the time of her illness they had a wonderful life together travelling extensively, eating out and enjoying the company of their long time mutual friends. I have asked myself a thousand times where or how did things go wrong for her? She had so much going for her. Both her sons and yes, even her grandchildren were doing extremely well in Australia, the love and devotion of a wonderful partner, a lovely home and, as far as I could see, nothing to worry about! Looking back so many things fall into place! I remember remarking how; during her last three visits to my home she hardly spoke a word. She was always going to visit her doctor with one thing or another, so much so I am ashamed I joked "If I went to my doctor as often as you do he would throw me off his panel telling me I was a hypochondriac!" Despite reassurance from her doctor he could find nothing wrong with her on three occasions she insisted on going to Bupa for a second opinion and was again found to have nothing wrong with her apart from stress. She was in the Saturday Hospital Fund. "They (the doctors) told Marie there was nothing wrong with her and she died of cancer" She always quoted this in reference to her best friend Marie who had attended her doctor for ages before she was indeed finally diagnosed with cancer and died some two weeks later.

I think she felt if they, the doctors had misdiagnosed Marie it could also happen to her! I do know she had, and has a great fear of cancer. There are so many things and indications we missed along the way! Not wanting to go to the planned meal for her birthday something she would normally have taken delight in. And, NO, she could not wear any of the many pairs of shoes she owned because they all hurt her, she would only wear a pair of "well past it" grubby slip- ons that normally would have been binned. It was only when she refused to eat that we knew something was seriously wrong. How sad and heartbreaking it is for us, her family to see Julia as she is now. To hear the expletives uttered from a lady who would not hesitate to reprimand a person she heard swearing. The aggressiveness that has come to the fore is completely alien to her character. We pray that in time our Julia will be returned to us, maybe not back to her complete self, although that would be wonderful but at least not having to see the look of terror and bewilderment reflected in her dear face when we look into her eyes. We hope this short history will be of some help to you but should you need to know anything else please do not hesitate to ask. In closing I should also mention we are aware that the staff are having a rough time in dealing with Julia. We are grateful for your patience and compassion.

Chapter Thirty One
Christ Church Bells

They headed down along the quays', four girls dressed in their best heading up towards Christchurch, the same as all the rest early, but yet undeterred, they hoped to find a spot that would give them an advantage over all those other Mots! "Imagine when them bells ring out" cried Maggie with a sigh, We'll get the chance to grab a kiss from every other guy! "A kiss would not be too bad" giggled ever charming Ella "But I hope to get me claws, into a truly permanent fella" "We'd have a better chance here, of finding true romance" "Than dancing round our handbags at some auld silly dance" "These fecking shoes are killing me, and the cost of them alarming!" "But, Jesus, it will be worth it if I find me auld Prince charming!" "Ya know yer sham from Gardner Street, the one with curly hair? Oh! God, I fancy him like mad and hope he will be there" "Are ya mad or what, have you forgot, he's only five foot seven? And those shagging shoes you bought make you five foot eleven! And then the quietest of the four, spoke up for the first time, "I'm here to relive old memories of someone else, not mine" "This is where my Ma met Da, all those years ago. He asked if he could walk her home as the bells rang sweet and low. Down through the years they told us kids of the hand that they were dealt, the struggles just to survive to find money for food and rent, yet despite it all their love survived through trial and tribulation, as strong and vibrant as the bells that rang out throughout the nation. And so for me I must confess, Christchurch will always be a special place, a sanctuary filled with memories. Let it's bells ring loud and clear for future generations and let each peel in its own way foster new relations.

About the Author

Though they could not see the back of me quick enough at George's Hill School in Dublin, I always loved my English classes. But my love of the English language and creative writing was very much restricted, firstly due to 'Irish' being our primary language, and then by a formidable nun who refused to believe that a girl like me, from the tenements, could possibly possess a gift for writing. The words that spilled from my imagination could not be mine, they must have been copied from elsewhere. The ruler was raised and my creativity was, literally, beaten out of me. I left school at fourteen and joined the work force as a machinist. Years later, I arrived in the north of England, married and had two children. I worked as a cleaner in the day and attended night school. I took and passed several 'O' levels and, in the process, rediscovered my love of literature and the written word. The tales in this compendium are drawn from my experiences as a child, growing up in the slums of North Dublin. They are slices of my young life, taken from a world now almost forgotten. Stories of family, filled with humour, warmth, wit and sadness that have tumbled from my distinctly Irish imagination. A young girl's reflections of life in the tenement blocks of Dublin and the lives of ordinary Dubliners.

Printed in Great Britain
by Amazon

35730544R00109